Also by Veronica Vera

*Miss Vera's Finishing School for Boys
Who Want to Be Girls*

MISS VERA'S

Cross-Dress

FOR

Success

A Resource Guide

for Boys Who

Want to Be *Girls*

MISS VERA'S

Cross-Dress

FOR

Success

VERONICA VERA

VILLARD ⓥ NEW YORK

As of press time, the URLs displayed in the text of *Miss Vera's Cross-Dress for Success* link or refer to existing websites on the Internet. Random House, Inc., is not responsible for the content available on any such site (including, without limitation, outdated, inaccurate, or incomplete information), and access to any such site is at the user's own risk.

Photograph of Miss Vera on title page by Annie Sprinkle

Library of Congress Cataloging-in-Publication Data
Vera, Veronica.
Miss Vera's cross-dress for success: a resource guide for boys who want to be girls / Veronica Vera.
p. cm.
ISBN 0-8129-9195-8 (trade pbk.)
1. Transvestism. 2. Transvestites. 3. Transvestism—Computer network resources. I. Title: Cross-dress for success. II. Title.
HQ77.V458 2002
306.77—dc21   2002023463

Villard Books website address: www.villard.com
Printed in the United States of America

468975

BOOK DESIGN BY JUDITH STAGNITTO ABBATE/ABBATE DESIGN

To the spirit of Mr. Lee G. Brewster

Acknowledgments

Throughout my years as a sex journalist, there have been many people from all parts of the transgender community who have trusted me with their stories. You have been my teachers. Thank you to the students and faculty of Miss Vera's Academy who make this work such a wonderful adventure and who give so much of themselves. And to all my sexy girlfriends, especially the ladies of Club 90, my female role models.

The staff at Villard have been consummate professionals in all departments—editorial, copy-editing, art, and publicity. I've felt supported every step of the way. They have transformed my manuscript into the very pretty package in your hands. (I just love my glam cover!) Thanks to Mary Bahr, who was there in the beginning. Thank you to Bruce Tracy, executive editor, who initiated the idea and then teamed me with my great editor, Tim Farrell. I could not have been in better hands.

Merci to Jamie K., who put his faith in me and opened his purse. I will cherish forever the memories of our sweet little academy mascots Archie and Ashleigh, who gave me comfort, and Phil, who gave me his all.

Veronica Vera née M. V. Antonakos
New York City, 2002

Contents

Welcome, student! (Photo by Miss Vera)

Introduction

elcome, gender explorer. Today is the perfect time for you to become the kind of woman you want to be. Transsexual, cross-dresser, drag queen, female impersonator, party princess . . . who are you? Perhaps you're a not a boy at all, but a girl who wants to be ultra-femme, so you've come in search of tranny secrets (of which there are quite a few). Maybe you are an academic with a dissertation on your inquiring mind. Some of you can be quite pesky and determined as you seek to understand what the age-old practice of cross-dressing means today and for our future. Perhaps you feel that your physical identity (sex) is at odds with your social identity (gender). Or that your partner preference (sexual orientation) is all over the map and you'd love some reassurance that you are not alone. Whether you are dressing up for Halloween or choosing a new lifestyle, crossing the gender border for a one-night stand or a permanent stay, no matter how you identify yourself in the ever-evolving tranny lexicon, you will find plenty of information here. This book is also about transforming your life in any way. We are all in a constant state of transformation, as is the world in general. The more you are aware of that, the more you can appreciate and influence the change. These lessons are about believing in yourself.

It gives me great pleasure to be your guide. I know a lot about life, both real and imagined. As dean of Miss Vera's Finishing School for Boys Who Want to Be Girls, the world's first crossdressing academy, which I founded in New York City (where else!) in 1992, I claim some authority. Hundreds of trannies have visited us from across the country and around the world. Thousands more have studied via my first book. The name of our school is recognized internationally. The students who visit us on campus are adult men, most of whom live very traditional lives, with jobs in the mainstream; about 60 percent of them are married. They spend anywhere from a couple of hours with us to a couple of days, immersed in classes with a faculty of deans who teach the students individually how to do their own makeup, walk in heels, go out and about town en femme, probe their erotic yearnings, network with others, and in general share and appreciate this part of themselves that has inspired them to dress in female clothing (usually in secret) since they were children. Their desire to wear women's clothing is a need to transcend the confines of gender, or "transgender." Many people besides academy students feel the need to transcend gender. When women felt it, we created the women's movement, and for every woman who burned her bra, there is a man ready to wear one. Like the big bang, these whirling male and female energies alive within each of us have given birth to a world and a culture that is the transgender movement.

Some people who transcend gender identify themselves as their opposite, male or female, and for others transgender has become its own location, not merely a temporary stop between male and female but yet a third option. Transylvania, as it was called so poetically by Frank-N-Furter of *Rocky Horror* fame, covers a large territory. Ten years ago, when I founded Miss Vera's Finishing School for Boys Who Want to Be Girls, I based your lessons on a philosophy of Venus envy, encouraging you with our school motto, *"Cherchez la femme,"* urging you to look *to* women for role models as you looked *for* the woman inside. I remain staunchly behind that directive and believe that this world is very much in need of massive injections of female hormones. To me, feminine ideals emphasize pleasure and tolerance. The "femmeself"—that amalgam of feelings and emotions that propels men to the academy in droves and inspires other gender explorers—is a reflection of the need for more emphasis on those ideals in society. That we get students from all over is evidence that this need is international. Further proof is the present sorry state of the world, which for too long has been dominated by testosterone. There is a crying need for balance.

At the academy we believe in "sissy power." I love that endearing term. My very first best friend, Carolyn, was called "Sissy" and her brother was "Skippy" . . . I know it's a bit much, but it was the fifties. I have taken pride in the sissies of the world. Today, the operative word is "tranny." I will introduce you to women who can be your female role models and encourage you to find more. You will also find tranny role models. The time has come to update your lessons and welcome those of you who are newly enrolled.

We'll begin with some basic definitions. A transsexual uses hormones and surgery to change his body. A transvestite, or crossdresser, changes only his clothes. Drag queens are gay. Female impersonators can be straight or gay, but they are professional performers and not turned on by their clothes (unless they are tight and sparkle). A person who is intersexed is born with genitalia of both sexes. "Transgender" is a relatively new and all-embracing term. The vocabulary grows.

But we are not going to get caught up with labels because definitions change very quickly and the lines between them blur. For instance, a transsexual can identify as such and never swallow a pill. A transvestite may experiment with hormones but not really want to make a permanent change. Straight men in drag (which sounds like a contradiction in terms but isn't) can be referred to as queens, especially by gay queens. "Cross-dresser" is a term used to describe straight men, though not all are. And women cross-dress too. "Transgender" is a good word except that it is not very sexy, which is exactly why some people prefer it. We are not going to spend a lot of time debating the terms. Debate is so male and boring! We have much better things to do—like progress and proceed. This book is about connections, not differences.

It's all one big tranny planet. There is no need for you to figure out where you fit in all this. If you are a tranny, you know you are. And if you are not, you can be, so don't be blue. Think pink! I prefer that you simply identify yourself as a student enrolled in Miss Vera's class. My goal is to increase your awareness of the options and encourage you to feel free to be. You can be a tranny without changing your body, even without changing your outfit. Our goal for an academy student does not stop when he looks and moves like a female but when he can take the lessons he has learned en femme and integrate them into everyday life, because freedom of expression goes beyond a fashion statement. Clothing is simply a prop, a very important prop, like one an actress might use to get more in touch with her role. At the academy, makeup and costumes are essential tools. I will show you how to use them. But the most important thing to change is your mind.

Consider this guide an academy field trip. You can wear your highest heels because your tootsies won't hurt a bit. I have included many websites because the Internet excels in precisely those areas of interest to the gender explorer: community, commerce, and sex information. The Internet can help you to connect with as many people as you choose and be totally out—or totally private. You can make friends, find galpals, or go for more intimate relations. Cybersex is safe sex—sex without physical contact—but the Internet can also help you to meet a partner (or two!) and get up close and personal. You can spend a lot of money shopping or you can build a file full of frocks and not invest a pretty penny, as I will show you. With the technology of the web there is a virtual supermall of goodies and services available at your lovely fingertips, so much, in fact, that you might find it difficult to sort through it all. That is where I come in. You can think of me as your gal Friday. I have put my expertise to use, browsing on your behalf, addressing your needs. I'll present you with lots of options to clothe your body, expand your mind, and fill your spirit. The choices are up to you.

No Tranny Is an Island

The real power of the Internet is that it enables people of like minds to go beyond geographical boundaries to form new communities or to discover communities they never knew existed. You and every other person who reads this book have become part of a community of gender explorers. You are also exposed to other communities I have chosen to include in this network: free speech activists, artists and entrepreneurs, admirable role models, friendly business owners. This networking has very far-reaching effects on our culture. We can form political lobbies, change laws; we can literally change the face, the voice, and the body of society. We already have.

It's in to be *out*! At the academy we like to say we put the clothes in your closet and let the girl out. In recent years, trannies have taken giant leaps forward into the mainstream. Awareness of violence and discrimination inflicted on trannies has increased. These hateful actions must stop. That is one big reason why I urge you to be out. If you are already out, good for you. I'm not surprised. Lots of people are doing it. Many of the sources listed in this book—from dress-up boutiques to legal aid to hair removal and more have been created by trannies for trannies. Trannies are doin' it for themselves. If you feel you still need some secrecy, then please be tolerant of others. Don't overcompensate by being a bully or a homophobe. That's so sad. And you'll miss out on the best parties.

Be a sister to every tranny. Please note, I said "every tranny," not "every tranny like you." There is no room for intolerance. Sissyhood is powerful. One of the main reasons the tranny movement has grown by leaps and bounds is the breakdown of barriers among its members. Though you may differ from one another in sexual orientation, you are united by your transgender and united even further by a preference for an alternative lifestyle.

So, students, I am suggesting that you have something in common not only with every tranny but also with swingers, S/M enthusiasts, lesbians, bisexuals, gay men, and queers of every persuasion—as many of you know, and more of you will discover when you take each brave step forward, whether you are mincing in stilettos or stomping in Steve Maddens. However you are dressed as you kick in the door of the establishment—no matter if you are adding body parts or taking them off, queen for a day or a lifetime. The courage that it takes to trust your heart is something all the world can applaud.

And the world is applauding you. From my academic perspective as dean of Miss Vera's, I see more and more trannies on the streets of New York. It is easier and easier to take our students in their lovely outfits to dressing rooms and ladies' rooms all over the city on field trips. When a retired general visited us, we took him to the costume institute at the Metropolitan Museum of Art and allowed him to pass through the armor collection in his new suit of clothes. As reported by the Gender Advocacy Information Newsletter (www.gender.org), trannies have become entertainment icons (transvestite comedian Eddie Izzard won two Emmys in 2000), athletic champions (the 1996 Thai national volleyball champions, basis for the film *Iron Ladies*), respected teachers (Deidre McCloskey at the University of Chicago, Miqqi Gilbert at the University of Toronto, and Jacob Hale at UCal, Northridge), and in other ways, pillars of society. In 1999, Dale Stewart, a student at Arlington High School in Indianapolis, won a court decision enabling him to wear a gown to his prom. This tolerance and understanding continues to spread and join with that of others who have chosen alternative lifestyles or those who support that freedom. Each of you is a messenger, a sort of traveling salesperson, like a Mary Kay rep changing the face of humanity. The world is more ready for you than you might imagine. Believe it. Be a tranny cheerleader. Society needs you.

The Art of Transformation

Life is art, and every tranny is an artist. The sooner you accept that about yourself, the happier you will be and the more others will recognize your artistry. You could have what you feel is the straightest, most boring job in the world. Caprice Bellefleur, one of the stars of *The Tranny School,* the British documentary about our academy, is a timid, bespectacled numbers cruncher by day. Weekday evenings, she blossoms into a disco diva. It does not matter; you are an artist. For what is art? It has been said that art is a lie that reveals the truth. Change your outer wear and you reveal the inner you. Shedding the fabric of social convention reveals the naked truth of the soul. Now multiply this by the idea that "no tranny is an island" and you can begin to understand how trannies can change the world. Where will all this lead? Trust your intuition. Wherever you are is okay.

Your class will be divided into lessons through which I will not only give you resources but also show you how to use them. In some, like the virtual boudoir, we will find items to help in your transformation—in other words, your school supplies. We will add to your sex education, study social and support systems and etiquette and netiquette, as well as address discipline problems, update med school and law school reports, and appreciate arts and entertainment. And life might spring a test, so study hard. You will be introduced to the faculty, other members of the student body, and visiting professors. Throughout, you will be guided to sources where you can find information for your continuing education and recreation. I have used true-life stories to illustrate different concepts such as sexual evolution and prove my points. The Patti Project continues the story of Pat, who was the thirty-eight-year-old male virgin I introduced in my first book. Patrick James is now Patricia Jane, a 24/7 woman of transgendered experience. Taxi represents the drag queens who were so determined to live their own lives that they uprooted themselves and planted new family trees. Colleen describes how she and her husband, Heather, make cross-dressing work within their marriage. Gayle's wedding is yet further proof that dreams can become real. These people have something else in common. They have grown and helped others to grow with them. Just as the people in these stories have lives that touch yours, so does your life touch others. A tranny by nature shakes up the status quo. You can also understand how some people, because they are afraid of change, protest it. That is why you need a fairy godmother to help you through this process, and that's *moi*.

I have been asked if I ever teach women to be men or drag kings. There is information for female-to-male trannies in this book, although it is not my prime focus. Some of the educational resources listed here, such as the International Foundation for Gender Education (www.ifge.org), do include information and links to female-to-male groups, a vital area of the tranny community. You can follow these links to people with far more knowledge than me on that subject. Or just start at Female to Male International (www.ftm-intl.org). My area of expertise is female development.

I have held the hand of many ladies in waiting who visit our school. I do this with the help of the academy's faculty of lovely and caring deans (www.missvera.com/faculty), all of whom are experts in their fields, and with the support of an energetic student council (most of whom would love to have my job). You can find out more about the herstory of our academy by referring to my first book (www.missvera.com/textbook), also entitled *Miss Vera's Finishing School for Boys Who Want to Be Girls*. (Let's face it, the name is genius and I thank goodness for the inspiration.) It is a great complement to your present course of study and recommended reading, if you hope to pass.

Even with all of this support and with one book already under my garter belt, I am still a bit daunted by the task at hand. The tranny movement has expanded so much and so rapidly in the past few years that I can't help but be humbled. But I will plunge forward because I have been asked and because I am not one to miss an opportunity—especially when there's shopping involved.

It is time, dear students, to accept the challenge of who we are. Why do I say "we," you might ask? I am not a drag queen, as was erroneously reported in the *New York Times,* and, as I have told countless radio jocks, "I am every inch a woman." I am a woman engaged in my personal evolution, just as all human beings are, and I am Miss Vera, a creature born of the imagination of Mary Veronica. Miss Vera is my femmeself; she is part of who I am. Miss Vera is my heroine, I think you can understand. Tranny is an attitude and, baby, I've got it.

That said, I ask you to light a pink candle and repeat after me: "I dedicate myself to releasing all of the juicy female energy inside me. I place my trust in Miss Vera's academy and my faith in the tranny movement. And I thank myself for this gift."

Cherchez la femme!

MISS VERA'S

Cross-Dress

FOR

Success

Miss Vera and the Deans (standing, left to right): Miss Kate, Miss Tiger, Miss Barbara, Miss Eva, Miss Deborah, Miss Melissa, Miss Mary Anne, Miss Vera; (seated) student Gayle (Photo by Nancy Rica Schiff)

CHAPTER 1

Faculty Tea

*D*ear Student, an invitation is extended to you to attend a tea party reception with the academy deans. This will be your opportunity to meet the teachers with whom you will study as you proceed on your journey to cross-dress for success.

We are all seated at a lovely, big, round table. It makes it so much easier to share a conversation. Miss Viqui and Miss Melissa are in charge of the tea service; these are our two etiquette experts. Miss Viqui is the voice you hear when you telephone the academy. And it is a lovely voice that she has, calm and reassuring and very polite, which is what she expects you to be. She sets the tone for your visit. We all understand that you are nervous (I prefer to think of it as excited). Miss Melissa, in her signature pillbox and early nineties Versace suit, takes a moment to compliment you on your outfit. Miss Deborah, our fashion maven and academy dean of cosmetology, has helped you pick out a pink suit with a peplum that gives you just a bit more flounce around the buttocks. Miss Deborah and I both love our pink suits. Hers is suede by Rena Lange and mine is Chanel and is festooned with gilt threads and gold trim. In fact, each of the deans is dressed in an outfit by her favorite designer (oh, it's so hard to pick, isn't it?). Miss Viqui is in a piece she saved from Willi Smith. Miss Barbara Carrellas and Miss Kate Bornstein, our "too tall blondes," are sizing you up and smiling. They can't wait to whisk you away to play. Miss Barbara is our dean of femmenergy and Miss Kate, our dean of hearts. Neither one believes in labels, except on their outfits. Miss Barbara will help you experience yourself as pure energy. She's a dynamo in her swinging bell-bottoms by Norma Kamali. Miss Kate was born a man and became a woman, but when that didn't fit, she decided to be neither, so she's a "gender outlaw," a term that sounds familiar because that is the title of one of her books, and it is in your pink-plaid book bag. She's a Betsey Johnson fan 100 percent.

Uh-oh, Miss Melissa, devil that she is, has asked you to pour Miss Eva a cup of tea. Oooh, I know it's quite a challenge, particularly since Miss Eva, our dean of seductive arts, has leveled her provocative gaze on you. I hope you've been paying attention to the pouring process. Miss Topaz, our dean of nightlife and newest dean, takes pity on you and whispers a reminder to use the tea strainer. Place it over the cup before you pour the tea from the pot. Your poor hands are shaking, and we can hear the clink as the lid rattles on the pot. Whew, success. You thank Miss Topaz. Miss Topaz, our East Village fashion innovator, combines slutty and classy in a wardrobe from Religious Sex, Trash and Vaudeville, and Daffy's ("Bargains for Millionaires"). She says she's a drag queen trapped in a woman's body, so she fits into our faculty perfectly.

"Is this your first visit to New York?" That's Miss Judy, our dean of voice. She's always full of questions. Miss Judy is an accredited speech therapist. Before her involvement with the academy, she had the least experience with our kind of girl, and she is totally fascinated and dedicated to helping you in your quest to sound more feminine. Putting voice to your emotions is so important. So she asks a lot of questions to hear what you have to say, to listen to the way you say it, and to give you instructions.

Miss Mariette Pathy Allen asks if you've ever seen yourself so totally transformed. For many of your sorority sisters who visit, this is the very first time they have been done up with such expertise. Miss Mariette will record this moment with her camera. She will be thrilled to lead you to what she calls "the dance of self-acceptance and self-creation" and to help you realize you are a three-dimensional person who can present herself in many ways. Miss Mariette likes to present herself in vintage Halston. For creating your portrait, she'd wear a pink-and-white vertically striped dress with pink buttons, pink belt, and shoulder pads. You, my dear, could wear several outfits, from baby to bride or beyond. Maybe you would find yourself in Miss Mariette's next book. Her first one, *Transformations: Crossdressers and Those Who Love Them*, is a classic. We've put it on your night table for bedtime reading.

The two deans who are having a bit of a private chat are Miss Tiger and Miss Maryanne Byington, our two movement deans. "I'd like to offer a suggestion, even at this early stage," says Miss Tiger. "I think our student needs to sit up a bit straighter. Your shoulders need to be back and down, my dear."

"Yes, tits up," Miss Eva, Miss Melissa, and I chant in unison.

"We'll work on that in ballet class," says Miss Tiger. "And just wait till you see the new outfits I've designed for our ballet students." We're all ears as Miss Tiger describes a "spandex jumpsuit, belted—that comes with a loose raglan-sleeve jacket that could also be a minidress, pants top, or robe—plus a knee-length chiffon wrap skirt that is worn over the jumpsuit when in class, and a Velcro head wrap. There is a simple version and a glitter version à la Cher in Bob Mackie."

"Oooh, very versatile," says Miss Viqui. "I like that." Miss Viqui, who is a mom with a five-year-old, likes to make the most of each minute. She is my deputy dean and helps me organize your schedule.

"No tutu?" asks Miss Melissa, attentive to ballet protocol.

"Of course, there is always the classic black leotard and pink tutu," says Miss Tiger, "but only if she is very, very good."

"Well, I'll put her in chiffon and feathers and rhinestone-trimmed high-heeled dancing slippers as I teach her to move backward across the floor in the arms of her dream partner," adds Miss Maryanne.

Your eyes light up as if you've just seen your first Barbie under your Christmas tree.

"Do you enjoy wearing high heels?" asks Miss Maryanne, half in jest. We all know the answer to that one. Miss Maryanne Byington has brought home trophies from many ballroom competitions. Her focus now is on teaching, and her goal is to help you to walk with confidence and grace. She says, "Sometimes the technique of rumba will create just the right walk for the right situation." Miss Maryanne loves to dance and dress in Oscar de la Renta's most colorful Latin-influenced festive party gowns.

"I'd like to know whom our student has picked as her role models," says Miss Eva. Miss Eva is quite formidable in Vivienne Westwood. Every question from her sounds like a sexy challenge.

Every academy student is asked to choose some female role models to help her as she strives toward womanhood. That is why our motto is *Cherchez la femme.* You seem to be a bit stumped. Well, I'll give you a little time to think about your answer. To help you along, the deans and I will share some of our role models. You can look them up to find out more about each one.

Miss Viqui says, "Shirley Temple Black, for her ability to get absolutely everything out of her childhood and then become an adult who was able to give back to other children."

Miss Mariette says, "I pick Gloria Steinem and certainly Margaret Mead. Mead was bisexual and a multitasker. She was a courageous explorer of gentler roles."

"I admire Mary Kay Ash," says Miss Deborah. "She believed in women and pink Cadillacs."

Miss Kate offers, "Audrey Hepburn and Morticia Addams."

"Oh, yes, Audrey Hepburn for me too," chimes Miss Tiger, "and Shirley MacLaine and of course the great ballerinas Margot Fonteyn, Alicia Alonso, and Cynthia Gregory. Also my eighty-nine-year-old mother, Margaret Farkas, the very most of all. Even with dementia and Parkinson's, she hasn't forgotten her manners and is as good-natured as ever."

"Here, here," and we clink our spoons to our teacups in honor of Margaret and all our moms.

"Well, I like Anne Francis," says Miss Barbara, "particularly during her stint as the adventure heroine Honey West."

"Hmm, I've always loved Emma Peel in that sense," I say, "but for a real woman, Victoria Woodhull, who had her own newspaper and was the first female candidate for president."

"And so far the *only* one," adds Miss Eva.

"Wait, I have one more. I'm not going to forget Jocelyn Elders, who told the country it's just fine to masturbate."

"Along that same line, I vote for Drs. Betty Dodson and Annie Sprinkle, our school sexologist," says thoroughly-up-to-date Miss Topaz.

Miss Eva, the activist, is back with "Emma Goldman." Miss Eva has contributed to various anthologies on sexual politics.

And activist Miss Melissa says, "Bella Abzug and all her hats and Judith Martin—Miss Manners—oh, and maybe Xena, Warrior Princess, for those difficult days." We all nod at that one.

"Well," says Miss Eva, "time to answer my question."

You wrinkle your little brow, your eyes light up, you straighten up in your chair, and you sing out, "My role model is Miss Vera."

Yes, that's what all you girls say. And I happen to think it's a very good answer. We're off to an excellent start.

Here, have a scone with marmalade and clotted cream.

Student Caprice Bellefleur
(Photo by Miss Vera)

CHAPTER 2

Your Boudoir

girl can never have too many drawers or closets. So when a neighbor of our academy informed me she had a dresser she no longer needed, I quickly offered to give it a home. Our own bureaus were bursting with panties, bras, and slips. Two of the building's porters moved the piece of furniture into our lovely pink space while I and Susan Sergeant, a former soldier and military attaché who served a tour of duty as my aide-de-campus, observed. Susan took a feather duster to the piece and placed a pink-and-white ruffled scarf across the top. "It turns me on," confided Susan, as she gazed longingly at the honey blond chest of drawers. "It reminds me of my sister's room. She would never allow me inside, so I used to visit on the sly."

Yes, a girl's room is a place of intrigue and mystery, a sanctuary. The academy is quite the feminine realm: elegant straight-back chairs, floral settee, crystal chandelier, flowing drapes all enveloped in a pink cocoon. Put yourself in a girl's world, and your surroundings will help support that frame of mind. Even something as simple and subtle as a vase of flowers can be inspiring.

How about you? Do you have a room of your own? Where do you keep your feminine finery? Maybe you are a princess who lives en femme 24/7 and your entire home is your castle. Some trannies reserve a single room in their home or rent a separate apartment for this purpose. Others, who may not enjoy such freedom, relegate their frillies to a storage locker, a hidden corner in the attic, or (boo-hoo!) the car. Even the most luxurious chemise can get pretty shabby when locked inside the trunk of a Plymouth, so you must remember to freshen up your frocks. The members of Crossdressers International, NYC (http://members.tripod .com/~CDINYC/) have their own apartment, a home away from home for those who pay to have keys and a place where, each Wednesday, the members host a drop-in social for those who would like to visit and primp. In California, Lydia's Transgender Fashions (www.lydiastv.com) offers storage lockers in addition to their transformation services. Where there is a will, there is a way—and when it comes to dressing up, a tranny is quite resourceful.

For our purposes, we will assume that you have a spacious and regal bedroom. Your bed is covered with satin sheets (www.silklinens.com). The mattress is thick, but, still, if a tiny pea were placed beneath it, you would feel it, my princess. You have an attached dressing room and a bathroom worthy of Cleopatra, with lots of room for you to accomplish the ritual of your toilette.

Fold or Fondle

A fun way to fill your closets and furnish the room of your dreams is by using the Internet. Let me explain. Have you ever clipped photos of hairstyles or dresses that you like from magazines? I know many of you have, because some students arrive at the academy with these tucked in their notebooks. It is so much faster and easier to do this clipping via the Internet. No scissors involved. I have a fantasy game I sometimes play when I receive a catalog via snail mail. As I flip through the pages, I ask myself, what would I purchase from this catalog if money were no object? Or—and sometimes better yet because of the delicious torture of having to choose—I ask myself, if I could pick out only three things from this entire catalog, what would they be? You can play this same game as you shop the virtual mall. I will lead you to some items, but as sure as Dame Edna is a drag queen, you will find yourself distracted in class, dashing off in different directions, as you see what else is offered on those sites. That is perfectly okay. Here, in Miss Vera's class, it is just fine to daydream—in fact, it is expected. But we do have a goal, so I suggest that as we shop you open some folders. You will want to have a reference library folder where you can put URLs of your new information sites. But the really fun part is creating a folder for each room or area of your boudoir. You can download the picture of the specific item you would like to add to your collection and put it in the appropriate folder—a folder for lingerie, for dresses, for earrings, for purses, for shoes, for cosmetics and beauty products. That way you can always come back to the item and imagine yourself using that $1,000 face cream (www.blissworld.com) or strutting around in those six-inch-heeled pumps (www.sexyshoe.com).

It's okay to browse without getting too organized. Aimless or anal, it's up to you.

You may want to make an actual purchase, depending on your needs and the contents of your purse. Remember, you pay extra to indulge in what I call the fondle factor—to hold it in your pretty hands, feel it on your skin, slip your pedicured foot into it. . . . I must also warn you that I have not tried all the products I mention, so I cannot give them the Miss Vera's Academy Seal of Approval, but I will let you know the ones I do personally recommend. As you try these products or services or discover new sites, I hope you will report back to me through our website (webhostess@missvera.com). That is your extra-credit assignment. You will be helping me and all your sorority sisters when you do.

La Toilette

A basic need for many of you ladies in waiting is removal of unwanted body hair. A visit to the International Guild of Professional Electrologists (www.igpe.org) gives basic information on the different types of hair removal, with emphasis on electrolysis. They can also help you find a practitioner in your neck of the woods through a link to the Electrolysis Referral Directory (www.electrolysisreferral.com). Be very careful about who you allow to wield the needle around your delicate features, whether they be above the neck or below the bikini line. Get referrals from satisfied customers. Here in New York City, Ms. Glorya Wholesome (www.glowgirl.com), Manhattan party hostess, says her enviable complexion is the handiwork of Richard at Richard's Body Beautiful (www.body-beautiful.com). Our webhostess Patricia Harrington gives her endorsement to Stephanie Fischman, a certified electrologist (C.E.) whose card reads ". . . because self-esteem is not a luxury." Miss Kate Bornstein (www.tootallblondes.com), our dean of hearts, recommends the speedy and intense procedures at Electrology 2000 (www.electrology2000.com) in Carrollton, Texas. I contacted Bren Piranio, a tranny who with her wife, Ruthann, co-owns Electrology 2000, a company in business since 1986. Bren explained, "Our practice now is mainly 'T' [transgender]. We have tailored our methods to get the job done as quickly as possible with minimal discomfort and maintaining quality results. . . . We usually have a person in for four to five days for the first clearing. We often will book two electrologists to reduce the client's chair time. Novocaine, administered by a staff doctor, makes the long sessions tolerable and comfortable. We work eight-hour days, yet you can only expect six to seven hours of actual production from each electrologist per day (they are human). The first clearing will usually get 40 percent of the total follicles on the face (active at the time), and the rest will cycle in at random over the next ten months. This is due to the genetic growth cycle all humans have. Each clearing takes less time than the previous one. If we can do a complete clearing once every six weeks, at the end of ten to twelve months you are done."

You might want to go back in a couple of years for one final treatment, but pretty much after that first year of treatments it's no more facial hair, forever. Not that you haven't earned it. As you might imagine, after four full days in the chair, you will emerge somewhat blushed. Says Bren, "You can expect some redness (pink) for one to three weeks from the first few clearings and less thereafter. Swelling lasts two to three days, and will also get less as the number of follicles decreases."

The hourly rate is $105 per electrologist per hour, and the average beard runs seventy to ninety hours to finish. First-time clearing may take thirty to forty hours for a cost of $3,150 to $4,200.

Laser hair removal is newer and therefore more controversial. Not all of the methods are yet FDA approved. But at Advanced Electrology and Laser Care (www.advancedelectrology.com), Dr. Mark Latina and Francine Capuzzo, R.N., use the FDA-approved GentleLase Plus laser and the Lightsheer Diode laser. Laser hair removal is not for everyone. The laser works only on dark hair, since it needs to focus on the hair pigment. For this reason, electrolysis usually follows the completion of laser treatment. Also, anyone with dark skin or a suntan cannot be treated because the laser light is absorbed by dark pigment and will be absorbed by the skin and not the hair.

Capuzzo estimates six visits spread over one to two years at $300 to $500 per visit to take care of full-face and upper-lip hair removal. This all depends on beard density, coarseness, and color. The charge is based on area, not time. But each visit takes about one hour. The darker the hair, the faster the process. Finally, a reason to be grateful for that five o'clock shadow!

Miss Vicky Lee, editrix and guiding spirit of *The Tranny Guide* (a must for your library: order from www.wayout-publishing.com) has made beard removal a personal project, keeping abreast of the latest developments. In issue eight she published a diary of her experience, including the emotional ups and downs, over nine monthly full-face laser treatments at London's Cristianos Clinic. Last year, in issue nine, she reported, "I am thrilled with the results." She summarized her monthly laser experience this way:

1. Day one: Treatment.
2. Followed by: five to seven days of rough skin that is hard to shave and is hard to cover with makeup.

3. Voilà: My wow day about ten to fifteen days after treatment.
4. Bliss: About two weeks of ecstasy—days of little makeup and super skin.
5. Challenge: In the last few days of the month some new follicle growth.

Those of you who want only temporary hair removal will be interested in a new spray-on product called Epil-Stop (www.epil-stop.com). As I write, this is being promoted via infomercials and over the Home Shopping Network. The makers promise that it smells like citrus. Let's hope so, because until now depilatories have been pretty foul smelling though effective. Another advantage is the spray factor. The less you have to touch a depilatory the better. The smell lingers worse than tired perfume. The roll-on version is made for small areas like lips and eyebrows, though I feel safer tweezing around the eyes or having them waxed by a professional.

Splish Splash

You know that I am really into bubble baths. Bubble baths help put you in girlie mode. It is where a lot of your relaxing beauty ritual takes place. And I want you to feel beautiful as you perform that ritual. Put on soothing music. We play the music of women during class at the academy when we perform transformations. Enya, Billy Holiday, Cecilia Bartoli, Annie Lennox, Alanis, and Sheryl are all popular here. But I prefer an Italian tenor in the bath. Brew a cup of ginger or peppermint tea to sip as you lounge. Ginger soothes the aches and pains of strutting in those heels. Peppermint calms the butterflies you might feel before (or after) a new adventure. It feels so nice to pamper yourself inside as well as out. A must is a pretty bath and shower bonnet. An enterprising young woman named Mimi agrees with me. She has created a line of essential but whimsical shower caps and other bath and spa accessories (www.mimialamode.com). Or you can choose to soak while wearing a waterproof turban, like a movie star of the forties (www.spaturban.com). Lean back on your bath pillow and indulge yourself. As a man, you are used to thinking in task-oriented terms, the goal of bathing being to get clean or wake up or both. So you opt for a shower. But women appreciate that relaxation is a goal in itself. That's one reason why we live longer.

I love to fill my tub nice and deep. If it is pedicure time, you can begin the process by removing old polish, clipping and filing your toenails while you draw your bath. Since my bathing pool (let's face it, "tub" is not the most glamorous word) is equipped with one of those overflow protectors, when the water and bubbles have reached the right level, I use a plastic lid made for this purpose to neutralize the overflow protector and keep myself in suds to my chin. This priceless item was discovered for me by the intrepid Susan Sergeant in Penney's hardware department. It is easy to add hot water after you have been soaking for five or six hours. Just kidding—a bubble bath is a leisurely process, though not quite that leisurely. Be sure to keep your personal tools within arm's reach. These include nail brushes for fingers and toes, an orange stick to push back those cuticles (so easily accomplished in the bathing pool), an exfoliating foot stick such as the Diamond Buffer (www.blissworld.com) to rid yourself of dry skin and calluses, and your triple-blade hand razor for shaving those legs silky smooth. When you are all finished, open the drain, stand, and shower off that pampered tranny bod.

Foot Fetish

Bundle into your soft terry or chenille robe and matching slippers and proceed to your dressing room. Remember, you have one, and it is nice and big and mirrored (think Versailles). There is a comfy chaise longue waiting for you (www.coxmfg.com), with a table and reading lamp next to *le chaise* so you can relax with a good book. But first, before anything else, you must cream your body. Candida Royalle, creator of Femme Erotic Video Productions (www.royalle.com), has the very softest skin because she creams it every day. Former high-class hooker Tracy Quan, author of *Diary of a Manhattan Call Girl* (www.tracyquan.net), recommends using lemon juice on the elbows. Lemon juice helps to exfoliate elbows and lighten dark skin. For legs, I recommend Mary Kay's (www.marykay.com) pedicure pouch. Everything you need is inside. But the best is the peppermint leg and foot cream. Rub it into your just-shaved legs and you will feel reenergized and frisky. As with the three ladies above, when I recommend women to you whose work I admire, I encourage you to find out more about each of them and consider them worthy role models. Candida Royalle is the foremost creator of erotic videos from a woman's point of view; Tracy Quan is not only an entertaining author but also a dedicated activist for the cause of prostitutes' rights, and Mary Kay Ash used beauty products to help women to feel good, not just by using the products but by selling them. Her goal was to inspire each woman in her sales force to increase her sense of self-worth, right along with her income. Plus who could not admire a woman who gave out pink Cadillacs!

Time to polish those toes. A word of caution re pedicures and manicures: Don't polish your nails too close to bedtime. Leave a space of about six hours. If your polish is even the slightest bit damp, rolling around on your satin sheets can take away the luster. While you wait for your toenails to dry, treat yourself to a book that will keep you in the femme mode. You can live vicariously as a stripper with my friend Lily Burana's *Strip City;* you can join the Grrl Genius Club (www.grrlgenius.com). Author Cathryn Michon says "To be a grrl genius, just declare yourself. No testing (IQ or genetic) is required." You can delve deep into tranny herstory with *Christine Jorgensen* by Anne Hooper or catch up with those Hollywood trannies in the latest issue of *Girl Talk,* edited by Gina Lance (www.girltalkmag.com).

Being glam requires constant vigilance. It's best to give yourself plenty of time so you are not rushed. Remember, Dianne Brill, a famous NYC girl-about-town of the eighties, wrote a book called *Boobs, Boys & High Heels, or, How to Get Dressed in Just Under Six Hours* and she wasn't kidding.

You do have the option of treating yourself to a salon manicure and pedicure. Most salons are very accommodating. The luxurious Bliss Spa in Manhattan (www.blissspa.com) is gender neutral when it comes to most of its services. In Manhattan, most neighborhood salons are under the proprietorship of Asian men and women, especially Koreans, or Russian women. Korean salons are often quite comfortably appointed. For your pedicure, you are seated on a large throne with whirlpool foot bath. Yummy. In our academy travels, we have found the warmest welcomes at Russian-owned salons. The Beauty & Youth Salon in Greenwich Village makes up for funky decor with enthusiasm for its tranny clientele. It's a great place to take a really nervous student. Anna Nikolla Salon on West 57th Street has put the polish on many an academy debutante. Our favorite manicurist is Amelia, though we love to hear Anna herself talk diet tips as she rings in the cash. It's great to go with a friend, especially if this is your very first salon manicure or pedicure. That way, she can take the pictures. Remember, if you document everything, you can relive the experience.

She's Got Game

Student Michelle George found a friend in Barbara Mirlocca, the fun-loving and talented image consultant and dress shop proprietress, co-owner of Florence's Fashions in Wakefield, Massachusetts. Barbara's shop is very tranny friendly. She transformed George, a fish-and-game warden, into Michelle, a young housewife, and took her on her first trip to a nail salon. Before long, Michelle was booking manicure appointments for herself in a salon closer to home. I cannot say this often enough: most merchants and service providers are thrilled to have your business, so don't be shy. When in doubt, call ahead. And be specific, don't hem and haw and beat around the bush. Try, "Hi, my name is George. When cross-dressed I use the name Michelle. I would like to book an appointment for myself as Michelle on Thursday of next week." There, that's not so hard, is it? In no time at all you will be that valued salon commodity, "a regular," and just one of the girls.

Why Long Nails?

Your hands are very easy for you to see. Beautiful nails are a constant reminder of the feminine you. They force you to make changes in your behavior that our verbal corrections to your table manners or other aspects of deportment are much slower to accomplish. When you lose an acrylic nail that has cost you $10, you will learn to be more graceful. Eating becomes a slower procedure. Dressing brings quite a challenge. The first time you are caught in the ladies' room unprepared, you will remember that your panties go over your garters and not the other way around. If you light your own cigarette and your nail goes up in flames, you will let that gentleman light your fire. Better yet, you may even give up smoking! Self-immolation is not the only danger associated with long nails: self-absorption is another. Don't get too wrapped up in your silk wraps. If you break a nail, it is not the end of the world. Remember, you are not your nails. And there are always Kiss 1 Easy Step Pre-Glued Nails at your local drugstore. Hooray for the Kiss company (www.kissusa.com). They have created artificial nails with adhesive already applied. Just pop them on and they stick and stay. These are a favorite of Imperial Court of New York's Empress XV Fiona St. James, the Latina Empress of Decadence and Style. Empress Fiona is quite the party girl, and in one weekend her nails need to withstand the equivalent of a month on *Survivor*. In order to remove acrylic nails, you must let your fingers soak in nail polish remover off and on for a half hour, not a pleasant prospect. With Kiss 1 Easy Steps, you can just pop them right off. If you would like to polish your press-ons to match your outfit, don't attempt it when they are already on your hands. Buy a roll of double-sided tape. Place it on a clean flat surface. Line up the nails in size position along the tape, leaving enough space in between for you to swish the brush, then polish and let dry. Kalina Isato (www.transvamp.com), an enterprising tranny with lots of great advice, reminds you that when a manicurist polishes natural nails in a salon, she does not polish all the way to each side. If you do the same, your nails will look more real than artificial.

We usually take our femme-intensive students, who stay with us for a few days, out for a manicure so they can have the ladies' salon experience. But if you are concerned about how you will look the next day when you lift a few with the boys, I advise you to opt for press-ons. To borrow a phrase that my friend Billie Bob the oilman likes to use when considering a drilling prospect, you need to consider your risk-to-rewards ratio. Decide for yourself. Are you willing to endure thirty to forty minutes of soaking in goop at removal time, if that's the price you must pay to spend a couple of hours in the Saks Fifth Avenue salon surrounded by the perfume, the gossip, the laughter, the presence of women, while you are pampered like any other femme fatale?

Student Heather and Miss Deborah, dean of cosmetology, go out on the town. (Photo by Miss Vera)

CHAPTER 3

Material Girls

art of learning to be a lady involves dealing with your manhood. Let's face it, the penis is a touchy subject. Well, that's not quite correct. Most of our girls prefer to pretend it is not there. Some will bring it out only as befits the occasion. A very tiny minority of prospective students are more preoccupied with penis manipulation than developing a persona. One visitor from Australia promised me that he had perfected ways of cock tucking that I had never seen. There was all this shaving and binding and surgical tape involved as he rallied round his flagpole and, actually, I didn't see the point. He had fetishized the whole procedure to the point of being boring . . . though certainly not to him. Well, he was from "down under," so I guess he took that seriously. When Dan Savage, author of "Savage Love" (www.thestranger.com), the syndicated sex column, asked if he could forward a letter to me, I was very excited by the idea of sharing my philosophies with his vast readership. Then I read the contents of the letter.

> Recently I was in a cross-dressing chat room discussing ways to conceal the male package. Someone came on and claimed that he could push his penis and testicles into his abdomen, totally concealing them. Knowing how much B.S. is slung around chat rooms, I doubted this was possible. Is it possible to insert the male genitalia into the body? If so, how is it done?
>
> Signed,
> Battling the Bulge

My ego went limp. Oh, yuck, more from the penis fetishists, I thought.

Please understand, I totally appreciate the power and pleasure of the penis. The penis is my friend. Even if the person to whom it is attached is somewhat cockeyed. Our academy ad campaign won very prestigious awards for our ad that read *Even the simplest evening gown can be ruined by a penis*. In presenting the Andy, an advertising award, to our ad creators, Joe Lovering and Jeff Griffith, the presenters admitted that they were thrilled to have the opportunity to say the word "penis" on the podium. Yes, the penis is fascinating, even when we don't see it, which brings me back to the subject of the letter.

I answered, "A lady in waiting can push his testicles up into his abdomen, then tuck his penis down and back between his legs, so that the scrotum envelopes it and forms what looks like a vulva."

Dan added in his own language:

Men's balls develop inside their abdomens before birth and drop into their nut sacks during infancy. After the balls drop, however, the little cavities in which they developed remain, and most grown men can pop their nuts back in. But popping your nuts back into your abdomen won't rid you of your scrotum, nor does it hide your cock. Unless that guy in the chat room was some sort of freak, I doubt very much that he could get everything—nuts, nut sack, cock—into his abdomen.

Thus, your testicles can be, shall we say, "squirreled away."

Once you are tucked flat, your pubic mound groomed by whichever method of hair removal you choose (or you might want to maintain a fluffy bush if you are a friend of the forest), you can use a tight thong panty, or a gaff, to hold everything in place. There are a few different kinds of gaffs available with new ideas always popping up. An item that I have my eye on is called the Panty-Up (www.frish.com). It holds the front flat and firm, while lifting the derrière to hopeful heights. Espy Lopez of Classic Curves (www.clcrv.com) offers a thong she describes as "the show-girl's secret." It is simple but effective, satiny and inviting. The idea is to wear a panty that will keep you flat in front but not squash your curvy buttocks. You can use a female's dance belt, too—but not a male's because that is padded—or the tried-and-true satin triangle available from Changes, the new tranny boutique in New York. Pop your testicles into their little abdominal cavities, tuck your penis down and back, let your scrotum caress your penis, then use the gaff to hold yourself in place. Or just wear lots of fluffy petticoats and you will be ready for whatever need might arise.

Breast Wishes

I have come to the conclusion that I am a breast fan. It is really no surprise because as a child I was turned on by the big-breasted heroines of the comic strips. I lusted after Daisy Mae and Tattoo, a femme fatale cohort in "Terry & the Pirates." Katy Keene (www.mystimemories.com) with her fabulous wardrobe was my ultimate role model, but Sheena, Queen of the Jungle, and those action babes with their low-cut, barely-there costumes got me very excited. I remembered all this as I went bra shopping on the net. While not all trannies wear bras, as we shall soon discuss, I know that most of you are at the very least interested in the subject.

First, let us discuss what goes into your bra. There are a number of ways you can create a bosom. You give yourself cleavage by bending over, pushing your breast flesh together in an attempt to make your nipples kiss. Granted, some of us have an easier time of this than others (meow), but even if you have very little breast flesh, this move will give you some cleavage. Drag actress Sherry Vine explains this in her delightful instructional video, *Teach Yourself How to Become a Drag Queen 101* (www.eastvillageproductions.com). You maintain that cleavage by taping around your chest using surgical tape. (Body hair should be removed *prior* to taping.) Instead of tape, you can use a Diva bra designed by the enterprising tranny Espy Lopez (www.clcrv.com). The Diva, which looks like the bottom half of a bra, can be worn on its own, or as a bra within a bra. Its purpose also is to squeeze your nipples together.

Most likely you will still want to give Mother Nature a hand by adding breast forms, either full-size forms or demis. There are all different kinds, ranging from cheap to expensive (www

.thebreastformstore.com). A homemade version can be made from a pair of panty hose, stuffed with bird seed. The knot that is used to tie off the nylon becomes your nipple. An exciting alternative, called the Miracle Bra, is sold by the tranny's friend, Victoria's Secret (www.victoriassecret.com). The Miracle Bra is filled with water. This is different from the WonderBra (www .wonderbra.com). WonderBra operates on the principle of squeeze and lift. The purpose of the WonderBra is to display maximum cleavage, so it's low-cut. If you are wearing full-size prosthetic forms, the WonderBra may not be your breast choice. For you, a cup with fuller coverage will help maintain the illusion of pulchritude, especially if you plan to remove your frock before an audience. The very latest WonderBra, however, is definitely worth a try. It's called airwonder and it comes with its very own pump, so you can enhance or minimize your curves as needed. This bra is lightweight and sounds great if you are a tranny who likes to sometimes feel heavy-breasted or pregnant.

I was very impressed with the bosom of student Michelle George, who wore a mastectomy bra. Mastectomy bras are not the most glamorous, but these are the bras of choice for more and more trannies. The cups are really pockets in which you slip the breast forms that conform to your body measurements. The results of such customized fits are usually very becoming. Michelle admitted she would not have picked D-cup breast forms if she were left to her own devices; but her specialist was right—these were the perfect size.

Michelle had telephoned ahead and explained her "situation" to the specialist at the same time she expressed her respect for the women who used the specialist's services following mastectomies. "She didn't have a problem fitting a man, though she had never done so before," said Michelle. "I brought an outfit to change into so I'd feel more comfortable being fitted. She was extremely thoughtful and sincere. . . . I even purchased a swimsuit from her after selecting the breast forms I liked. I was told to feel free to call anytime. She said that rather than advertising for a male clientele, she preferred to make exceptions for "special cases" on an individual basis and that I had been a "perfect lady."

Michelle handled herself beautifully, and I encourage you to follow her lead. Though her cup size is D, her grade is an A.

Why not return to those thrilling days of yesteryear and your own magic bullet? Bra, that is. The retro bullet, or torpedo, bra is a lethal weapon and it is still available from a Canadian company called Cameo Intimates Lingerie (www.cameo-intimates.com). They even have open-nipple bullet bras and, yes, these are as sexy as they sound.

I'd like to call your attention to a relatively new fashion statement, the exposed bra strap. This is a relief, especially for zaftig women and trannies. Now you don't have to forgo that spaghetti-strap dress for fear that if you wear a strapless bra, your boobs might fall out. More good news is the option of invisible (transparent) straps, an idea that took a long time coming. You can get a plunge bra with invisible straps (www.braexperience.com) or just the straps themselves, a mere $6 well spent (www.tinyshop.com). All of this from those dedicated folks in the field of bra research and development who constantly strive to give us girls uplifting support.

The Big Squeeze

Undergarments have been with us in one form or another throughout history and have been the subject of museum exhibitions. The garment with the firmest foundation, both literally and figuratively, is the corset. Ancient Egyptians were among those who wore them. We carry on that tradition at the academy. We ordered them so frequently from my dear friend Ms. Antoinette at Versatile that she offered to make up a special Miss Vera Tranny Training Corset, as well as reprint the classic *Figure Training Fundamentals* (www.missvera.com) for instruction and edification. Corsets from Versatile were used in the movie *Moulin Rouge* (www.moulinrouge.com)—a must-see for any of you cancan devotees. Be sure to have smelling salts nearby because you could faint from overexposure to corsets and crinolines.

Corset critics have argued that the garment is physically dangerous or an instrument of female subjugation or both, but corset fans are legion and they are quite organized. The Long Island Stay Lace Society (www.staylace.com) lists a number of national and international gatherings, many of which take place annually. The society's founder, Tom Lierse, is always ready to give a hands-on demonstration. I once experienced a lacing up from Mr. Lierse, and I can tell you the man has a serious (gasp!) commitment to his work. Corset training is offered through Ann Grogan's Romantasy Boutique (www.romantasy.com), a San Francisco institution. But, I warn you, if you are hoping to break any records, you've got a long way to go. According to an article in the *National Enquirer*, the teeniest waist on a living person belongs to a young lady named "Spook," who measures in at 14 inches. Until recently, Cathy Jung held the record with 15 inches. And neither one of them measures up to the late Ethel Granger, still the champ with a mere 13½ inches. Coincidentally, that's the same number of inches as claimed by the late John C. (Johnny Wadd) Holmes for a different section of the human anatomy.

I Love You, Butt

We're down to the bottom line. If you are one of those lucky girls with a bubble butt, you may move on to the next chapter. Or if you prefer to go au naturel and not be encumbered by extra layers, move on. But if you would like to fill out your miniskirt to the max, you'll need some padding. This is one area where you really must experiment. There is a very common, little padded panty that has been around forever and looks pretty terrible. You know the one I mean—it has pads at the sides and back, but they are not positioned in a way that is realistic. The incomparable Espy Lopez Classic Curves has designed a butt that, I am happy to say, she named the "Veronica." It comes in two versions: one with thighs and one without. Espy's products were used in the movie *To Wong Foo* . . . and being behind Patrick Swayze's butt is quite a claim to fame. The Veronicas are very realistic, though they are pretty formidable . . . which I guess makes them all the more real, at least in the case of this Veronica. You might like to sculpt your own bottom or buy individual foam inserts (www.cpmart.com) and slip them into your panty hose or tights at the right spots. The Panty-Up that I mentioned previously has potential because while just lifting your butt and not padding it, you're still left with plenty of jiggle room, which is a very important asset.

Student Jean Katz at Lee's Mardi Gras. She's eighty-eight, but thanks to the academy doesn't look a day over seventy! (Photo by Miss Vera)

CHAPTER 4

Honor Roll

hopping is fun, and no one understood that better than Mr. Lee G. Brewster. So get comfy and pour yourself a glass of wine or brew a cup of tea while we take a moment to stop and give credit where credit is due.

Among the first questions members of the tranny community asked when I told them about this resource directory was "What are you going to say about Lee Brewster?" One of the reasons people ask is because we all miss Lee so much. We want to hear his name and remember him and remember that feeling we had when he was alive. Mr. Lee G. Brewster is at the top of the honor roll. Lee, of course, was the owner and founder of Lee's Mardi Gras Boutique, the world-famous tranny department store. But the store was more than a shopping center. Lee was not simply a retailer. Lee's Mardi Gras was a glittering oasis where those who were thirsty for glamour, for fun, and most of all for freedom could sip till their B, C, or D cups ran over. The business was a creative work of art from a former party hostess who was a political activist. As his friend and colleague Ms. Bebe Scarpi so eloquently states, "Lee G. Brewster was the mother of us" (www.inch.com/~kdka/leegbrewster/inmemoriam.html).

The first time I visited Lee's Mardi Gras, the shop was located on 10th Avenue at 42nd Street, on the second floor above a liquor store. I climbed the steps and entered a space entirely—and I mean entirely—filled with feminine frillies, tranny accessories, wigs, shoes, dresses, lingerie, and tables and shelves filled with books and videos. Patrons had to move single file through this maze, sometimes meeting a pussycat along the way. The cramped quarters made the place all the more exciting. You never knew whom, wearing what, you might encounter around the bend. Presiding over it all was Lee, so soft-spoken and quiet, dressed down and wearing that funny toupee. At the time we met, I was just beginning my life in sex research, having returned from a course of study in the chambers of my then new friend Ms. Antoinette, who had introduced me to Lee. I asked Lee if I could interview him for Antoinette's magazine *Reflections*. Fortunately for me, Lee, who could be quite fussy about such things, agreed. That interview alerted me that this was a man who deserved my respect. Lee G. Brewster was a tranny to be reckoned with. He was one of the people—if not *the* person—who got the New York City law against cross-dressing abolished. Lee never tooted his own horn, but I know he appreciated the article I wrote and the credit it gave to his achievements.

A few years later, when Lee moved his store to the huge loft at 400 West 14th Street, I was thrilled. My apartment was just one block away, and even before I started the academy, Lee's became my favorite personal lingerie store where I could always count on finding just the right see-through something in a pinch. My only frustration was that except for the marabou-trimmed slippers, not one pair from Lee's tantalizing wall of shoes was smaller than size 9. I guess that was only fair. After all, I had the whole city in which to shop for high heels, but the whole city did not have Lee's taste in bows and glitter in widths that could accommodate a real foot and at such reasonable prices.

Once I started the academy, I had a lot more reasons to visit Lee's Mardi Gras on my own, with my girlfriends, or with students and sometimes a television crew trailing behind me that Lee had graciously agreed to allow "as long as they mind their manners" and did not disturb his customers. I always spent more time in the store than I planned because I liked to gossip with Lee. "Do you know that some of these so-called straight cross-dressers are doing each other," he confided, his voice rising an octave into that Southern drawl. Lee grew up in coal-mining country, but I always pictured him dressed like Miz Scarlet (but with the heart of Miz Melanie) in an antebellum gown. When his beloved Kitty Cat had to make a trip to the pet hospital's emergency room, Lee was outraged at the staff's cash-before-comfort attitude. Kitty Cat was in the treatment room, and Lee was very upset, for he loved his kitties to pieces and had been waiting for some time for information. Before the staff would let him see his pet, they demanded payment. Lee was incensed. "I threw my platinum American Express card down on the desk and said, 'Kitty Cat is no pauper!'" Lee believed in simple kindness.

I have a lot of gifts for which to thank Lee. Some were tangible, like a pair of white lace crotchless panties I had picked out to entertain a lover or the magic wand I hold in my fairy god-mother photo. Lee hostessed the party for my first book signing. His assistants gave the shop a glamorous pink makeover and served champagne. When Bebe told me that Lee was in the hospital, I visited him and brought him some peonies, his favorite flowers. He was not pleased to be there and chose to leave us, making a graceful exit just a few days later. In a way, his job was done. He had given good service. Lee made his mark on the world and on so many of us in it. He did not merely bring cross-dressing out of the closet, he brought it into a five-thousand-square-foot palace. Not an easy task with the high costs of Manhattan. Lee paid $8,000 a month in rent alone. That's a lot of wigs and falsies. It was a tremendous financial responsibility that Lee bore mainly because of his commitment to the tranny community. Mr. Lee was petite, but she had very broad shoulders.

Not long after Lee's death I was riding home on the crosstown bus. As I prepared to get off at my stop, I looked straight down the block to the place where Lee's Mardi Gras used to be. Suddenly, I felt I was on the edge of a cliff. There was a big emptiness in the pit of my stomach and I realized how safe in my work I had felt when Lee had been there. For that I will always be grateful. I am proud to have known him, and I will never forget Lee G. Brewster or the values that he held dear. In or out of sequins, he set a shining example.

Student Lisa in everyone's favorite dress—
red sequins and just the right length!
(Photo by Miss Vera)

CHAPTER 5

Your Wardrobe

A s much as clothes make the tranny, trannies make the clothes. Fashion is an art and tranny is its muse. The relationship between you and your dress is dynamic and dangerous. Like Kali, the goddess who is creator and destroyer, you shake up the status quo yet keep fashion alive. Take a look at television. One of the most popular designers today is Patricia Field (www.patriciafield.com), who designs the wardrobe for *Sex and the City*. Before Sarah Jessica Parker was decked out by Pat Field, the House of Field was the place for club kids, especially trannies, to shop. The two Field shops in New York City—the original Eighth Street store and Hotel Venus on West Broadway—are filled with tranny essentials: boas, rhinestones, and club wear that defy gender. In San Francisco's Haight-Ashbury, the Piedmont Boutique (www.piedmontsf.com) is as cutting edge as it is retro with wild colors, spandex pants, and stripper gear . . . tossed into the spin cycle, and, of course, in both places wigs, wigs, wigs—the tranny party hat. *Moulin Rouge*, the fashion movie of the moment, brings back corsets and crinolines so that Antoinette at Versatile, whose company was founded on a firm tranny foundation, is now selling wasp waists to Bergdorf's and Victoria's Secret. Fashion never forgets and neither does a tranny. Your clothes are connected to your memories. They are lifelines to your emotions. By making your fashion choices—putting them out there for all to see—you celebrate who you are and where we've been, and you ensure the survival of the species in whatever form and whatever fashion.

Girlfriends

Are you ready to go shopping? It's always more fun if you take a girlfriend along to help you make those difficult decisions—like shall I buy this dress or pay my rent? Miss Deborah, our academy shopping maven, is an expert in such areas. If you are going out en femme and are even the least bit trepidatious, a girlfriend will help calm your nerves and make sure your titties don't bounce on the dressing room floor. If you are shopping in male drab for your femmeself, a girlfriend will encourage you to try things on when you might not think you can, and help with sizes. Remember to always bring a tape measure with you. It's a great help for measuring sleeves. You may be one of those girls who is unafraid to enter any store en femme. I hope that you are, for you really do have the world on your purse strings. Merchants want to make sales, and almost everyone will treat you with the same respect you treat yourself. If they do not, shop elsewhere.

Tranny Specific

Among the places that are the most fun to shop are stores that cater mainly to trannies. When dear Lee Brewster was alive, Lee's Mardi Gras was my favorite shopping experience. I could always find a great gift for a nontranny girlfriend or for myself as well as outfits for our students. In New York, besides Pat Field's shops there is Changes, a teeny tranny boutique that shows great promise. The owner, Leslie, is a tranny with excellent taste. San Franciscans can shop at the Foxy Lady Boutique. L.A. girls have Lydia's TV Fashions in Sherman Oaks, Versatile Productions in Orange, and Jim Bridges' Boutique in North Hollywood. Reno offers trannies the ten-thousand-square-foot Romantic Sensations run by Jerri Lee, publisher of *Transformations* magazine. Girls with something extra in Michigan can find what they need in Clinton at Ms. Lisa's shop, the Dressing Room (www.mslisasdressingroom.com). In Auburn, Massachusetts, there is the Glamour Boutique and in Wakefield, Florence's Fashions. Dream Dresser in Washington, D.C., and Fashion Fantasy in Manassas, Virginia, make sure that our well-heeled senators and congressmen never have far to go to find their maids' uniforms. Oh, yes, and then there are the shoe stores and wig shops and more that are listed in my Resource Directory. Girl, you better work!

Your Shopping Profile

Yes, there are plenty of shops for you to visit, tranny specific and otherwise, but the big tranny shopping mall is the Internet. Let's talk about the psychology of shopping online. Are you a department store deb or a boutique babe? Do you like to find everything in one place or prefer to search for specialty shops? To answer these questions we must consider different factors. The factors are affected by what you need and for what purpose. Let's say that you are putting together an outfit for a party. Without even considering what dates you may have in your personal circle, there are *so* many events on the tranny calendar: drag balls, transgender conventions, fetish frolics, Halloween, Mardi Gras . . . a girl can keep busy every weekend of the year.

The first factor to consider is time: Are you shopping last minute on impulse or for an event still two months away? Be sure you can get what you want in the time that you have. You can't wear a picture to a party. A site such as the aptly named Versatile Fashions offers everything under one big hoop skirt—from your gown to your shoes to your bra and the bosom that fills it, and much more. Yes, the hoop skirt, too. Versatile's designs are for the exotic lifestyle, so a bit more than a "mother of the bride" might choose. It's not likely that you *are* a mother of the bride, but these days you never know. You can always shop JC Penney (www.jcpenney.com), which also has everything you need, including breast forms, padded panties, and shoes up to size 11. Another one-stop surfing site is owned by Jim Bridges (www.jbridges.com), who went from makeup artist to minimogul. Jim brings a dash of Hollywood and Las Vegas to his enterprise. Both Jim and Antoinette have spent years building fine reputations within the tranny community. It is an excellent idea to support the merchants who have supported you. Believe me, these people are not in it simply for the dough. You girls know that a tranny can be a lot to handle. You have a reputation for endless chitchat. Your phobias can be exhausting. You can be quite anal in your desire for perfection. It's all part of your charm. I remember the day after the death of Lee Brewster. Some of Lee's employees were in the store as a matter of habit. They were in shock and gravitated toward the place that had been and was still such a big part of their lives. They wanted to be together. I walked one block over to be with them. The phone rang, and it was a customer who needed information. He was told that the owner of the store had just died and they were not really open for business. This tranny was undeterred and continued to ask a ton of questions about the right size for this and that. Finally, Miss Bebe took charge and stated flatly that the store was closed and they were in mourning. "Does this mean I can't order my corset?" We all laughed because the caller's behavior was no surprise and no one would have understood that better than Lee. A tranny can be a bit self-centered. She can also be the most generous and community minded, as proved by the growth of the tranny movement. I am particularly proud of our academy girls who constantly show me the very real hearts beneath their faux bosoms.

Some retailers take longer to deliver merchandise than others. You don't want to be biting your acrylics down to the nib. Shop only at sites that supply e-mail addresses and/or phone numbers, so that you can follow the progress of your order. Why not contact them before you make a purchase to check on their response time. Deal only with merchants who offer secure servers. Also you don't want to find yourself face-to-face with someone in a dress identical to yours. So consider the likelihood of that happening before you make your purchase.

Privacy is another factor for the modern-day tranny. You may feel more comfortable dealing with one merchant that you know maintains a policy of discretion rather than some unknown who may publicize your favors like a barroom tart on a bathroom wall. Still, these days who does not get unsolicited mail? Spam is more the rule than the exception, and you can use that to your advantage. If you need to cover your tracks, you can always claim ignorance or that someone must be playing a joke on you. I don't know how many calls we receive at the academy from policemen, firemen, or stock traders who tell us they are responding to our signal to their beepers when we have made no such communications. Usually it is their best buddies playing jokes on them. I have to think there is something to this wealth of interest. There is much truth in jest. In fact, so many of these bewildered callers were members of New York City's finest that I wrote them offering to organize a policemen's ball. The offer still stands.

Clothes Lines

This is a special message to anyone who has ever stolen a bra or panties from a clothesline (you know who you are). Many times students have confided to me in letters like the following from which I will take a brief excerpt.

> I am one of those men you hear about who likes to wear women's underwear, primarily panties but occasionally garter belts, nylons, and sometimes slips and nightgowns for lounge and sleep wear. . . . My first recollection of my attraction to women's underwear was at about age four. I remember my mother and a friend bringing in the laundry while I watched. It was very warm and they had stripped down to their bras. I took a pair of my mother's panties and put them on. They laughed. . . . At about eleven years old, I resumed the masturbation practices. [He had begun years earlier.] I reached puberty at about age twelve, and was then able to ejaculate. I was always concerned that I would ejaculate on my mother's panties and

get caught using them to play with myself. . . . Instead, I would steal panties from neighborhood clotheslines.

Such confessions are not unusual. What I want to tell you is that, as an adult hearing these stories, I always thought that a kid who stole undies from a clothesline was really cool. I admire the determination of children to be who they are, no matter how much they are put down for it. So if you were one of those kids, I say, good for you. It was society that was wrong, not you. Plus, I very much appreciate the delightful feeling of pleasuring oneself through silky panties, or soft cotton Carter's, as I myself did as a child. There are one or two items in my lingerie closet that still rub me the right way. As for the moral issue of stealing . . . was Jean Valjean guilty for stealing a loaf of bread?

Welcome mat. When you are an adult, no such imprimatur applies. Adults go shopping. Most lingerie store owners welcome your business. Many of them telephone our academy and ask for our brochures to pass on to their clientele. I asked Sandi Simon, owner of Frishman's in the Bronx (www.frish.com), to make a contribution to this book. She wrote:

> As a sixty-nine-year-old bricks-and-mortar business catering to women, we are delighted to be serving men. In 1997 we went online, hoping to help the women of the world with girdles and bras. Our e-mails were full of queries ending with initials hitherto unknown to us, CD and TG. After our first Men's Night it has been one long romance. Three and a half years later we have a healthy following in the CD community.
>
> We are stimulated and intrigued by the varied makeup

of our CD and TG customers and are continually curious as to what makes them tick. . . .

Sandi issues a gracious invitation: "Please come to our store which has been referred to as the 'Great Cross-Dresser Candy Store.' Browse our five thousand square feet of products, only a few of which are on the net, and be pampered by our friendly staff and talented seamstress."

Sandi leaves no doubt that her company has spread out the welcome mat, as do proprietors across the country and around the net. Remember, the same rules of etiquette apply whether shopping online or in person. Act like a lady, even when dressed like a gentleman, and be considerate of the other person's time.

Slinky toys. I happen to love negligees and sexy night-gowns, so I set out to find peignoirs in cyberspace. What tranny has not been to Victoria's Secret or Frederick's of Hollywood? But I was after delicate silks and satins, not easy-care polyester. I visited the La Perla site (www.laperla.com), which is more an on-line showroom than for retail shopping. It is quite hypnotic and recommended for voyeurs but did not help in my quest. A number of British companies offered beautiful designer gowns at a queen's ransom but only in sizes up to 16, which appears smaller than U.S. size 16. So they might not fit your actual body, but they can fit the girl who lives in your virtual boudoir. Another British site (www.luciaclark.com) offers plus-size gowns in silks and satins. And Iris Silks (www.irissilks.com) in New York offers plus-size silk chemises and kimonos.

At Secrets in Lace (www.secretsinlace.com) owner Dan Whitsett told me they increase their supply of silks at holiday time. Meanwhile, the site carries lots of very sexy and classy lingerie, much of it their own private label and in sizes from petite to plus. The Whitsetts truly love lingerie and will travel the globe to find just the right nylons, just the right gloves, to add to their catalog. When I met Dan in New York I presented him with a vintage bustier that I owned in the hopes that he might create a modern copy. It was as if I was passing on a family heirloom and in a way I was. It even felt still warm. The bra was already vintage when it was discovered by my friend Gloria Leonard. It graced her bosom in a few X-rated movies. The bra was a long line, a combination black net and black satin and heavily boned, a most reliable strapless. I snapped it up when Gloria was having a tag sale before moving to her Hawaiian paradise where she planned to wear only a lei of orchids and a bikini bottom. I had put it to good use, wearing it in erotic photo shoots and on special occasions at home, but now it was in need of repair. Perhaps Dan could bring it new life. I would love to see it offered to all of you girls to wear. Treasured garments and great designs deserve long lives.

Accessories Department

Certain articles of clothing go a long way toward making a boy feel like a girl. A pair of panties, a bra—these exude a powerful allure, and so do shoes, the most provocative being high-heeled sandals that strap at the ankle. (You may already be excited simply reading that description!) Without a doubt, these are the most popular shoes in the academy wardrobe and favored by trannies worldwide. I'd like to take a moment to analyze this style. First, there is the openness. Your toes, usually unseen, are exposed (please, make sure they are polished). The viewer experiences a tiny shock as his eye is immediately drawn to them. If you happen to find yourself in a kinky nightclub, your exposed instep is a foot fetishist's heaven, so inviting to a worshipper's tongue. You do not slip into this shoe, it wraps around your foot, and the strap reveals a kind of bondage. Unlike pumps, once you have strapped yourself in, you cannot slip your foot right out, say, to make an escape from danger or discovery. You have made more of a commitment. Everyone is aware that this style is erotic, so in wearing them, you are saying, "I am not afraid to be sexy." And that is a very good thing.

Now that you've got the world at your feet, it won't take long before they are checking out your legs, and I know how proud of them you are. When wearing stockings, be sure to wear sandalfoot nylons to complement this look. I was very happy one day when I found a pair of ankle-strap sandals at Payless, size 11, for $12.99. Yes, girls, you can shop at Payless, where sizes go up to 12 with many in wide widths.

Recently a student asked me to order a pair of red sandals with ankle straps and four-inch heels. I found the shoes online at www.sexyshoe.com. As she planned to dance the night away, I questioned whether such a challenging heel was the right choice. She reminded me that four inches is not that high when your shoe size is 14. Do the math and you will understand.

The phrase "slave to fashion" is nowhere as appropriate as when it refers to shoes. For modern girls like me, shoes stir emotions of love and hate. On a recent trip to Manolo Blahnik, I fell in love with a pair of pumps, but those pointy toes stopped me from consummating the relationship. You can help spearhead the campaign for wider shoes. Your feet are bigger and wider. Buy more shoes and perhaps manufacturers will get the message to create attractive shoes in wider widths. This will help ease the torture of all of the women of the world.

Handle with Kid Gloves

Once you go above size 8, ladies' gloves are hard to find. The typical tranny glove is one size fits all and made from satin spandex and available all over the map. But they are for indoor use only. If you want to show off your manicure, opt for the fingerless version. Fishnet gloves are fun and much more sexy and let your press-ons show through (www.greatlookz.com). What's a girl to do when there's a chill in the air? Stretch velvet will keep you covered and warm and will stretch to fit. But it's leather gloves that give you that air of glamour and mystery while keeping you relatively warm. (Okay, so you have to give up a bit of heat to be glamorous, but you get it back in other ways.) My search for leather gloves in big-girl sizes led me to Jay Ruckel, master glovecutter at La Crasia (www.wegloveyou.com). Jay told me that he custom-makes ladies' gloves for men all the time. He said that a few years ago, when the Federated chain of department stores was in financial trouble, custom work from trannies helped save La Crasia's business. He's been making gloves for over thirty years and is so dedicated to the craft and the preservation of its history that he's started a glove museum and has been taking graduate courses at New York's Fashion Institute of Technology under fashion expert Valerie Steele. Jay made the white gloves that Julia Roberts wears on her shopping spree in *Pretty Woman,* and just before the attacks of September 11, he made a similar pair for a gentleman who was also a jet fighter pilot. The man approached Jay after the glover made a presentation at a military museum. "I thought of him up there piloting the plane, maybe even wearing those gloves, and thought, he's up there protecting us—let him do it naked if he wants." I agreed with his sentiment, but told him the fighter pilot would, no doubt, much prefer the rest of Julia's outfit to go with the gloves.

To have gloves custom-made, Jay offers these measuring instructions: Make a fist and then measure the distance around your knuckles, excluding your thumb. Measure from your wrist up your arm to the length that you want, then draw an outline around your outstretched hands. On the same page as your handprint, mark off three inches on a straight line. Then fax the info to Jay. Faxes sometimes shrink and the ruler measurement helps with accuracy.

Hats On

Just because you are wearing a wig, you are not prevented from wearing a lovely chapeau. Bitz N Pieces wig salon has hats in larger sizes. If you'd like something more romantic, Ellen Christine will custom-make it for you. You can walk into her lovely shop in Manhattan and be surrounded by hats, both modern and vintage, or order online (www.ellenchristine.com). She'll do custom work too. You can have your very own Easter bonnet with all the frills upon it and you'll be the grandest lady in that or any other parade.

Channel your desires. There is stiff competition for your shopping dollar. Perhaps the most irresistible merchandise is sold via TV at the Home Shopping Network (www.hsn.com) and QVC (www.qvc.com) and more. When I saw and heard these programs for the first time, I recognized that this medium was perfect for you girls. Most of the items are sold in a wide range of sizes. Need a leather skirt in 3X? It's there for you and in your choice of three colors. A cubic zirconia engagement ring in size 10, no problem.

You can go online to buy, but I challenge you to make full use of TV shopping by calling up with the aim of being heard on the air. Wouldn't you just love to have a little chat with well-known celebrities like Suzanne Somers, Joan Rivers, famous designers like Bob Mackie and Nolan Miller, or the network hostesses like Colleen Lopez and others like her who have become stars because they know how to be good girlfriends? I once heard a caller named "Margaret" wax enthusiastic to Joan Rivers about how much she loved her recent bejeweled acquisition. Hearing the voice of this "Peggy" I suspected she might also pass for "Pete." Joan did not even bat a false eyelash—she just kept hustling those products.

Crystal lass. While watching QVC, during a Nolan Miller program, the item for sale was a diamanté bracelet, but it was not the bracelet that caught my eye, it was the gorgeous negligee that the model wore. Mr. Miller referred to the negligee. "Oh, that's the one I designed for Linda Evans in *Dynasty*. I designed lots of negligees for *Dynasty*." I checked the QVC website (www.qvc.com) in hopes that the negligees would be offered for sale. There were just a few and they were offered in a special auction. I hope that Nolan Miller does a *Dynasty* tribute collection. If he does, I'll be the first online. Here at the academy we are addicted to negligees. Each of our deans has her own in a different style and a different shade of pink. Imagine yourself as you sit in our makeup chair, your body, too, wrapped in satin, a pampered princess in the lap of luxury.

Oh Boy, eBay! There is another shopping option. With this one, you may need the help of lady luck since eBay (www.ebay.com) is an online auction house—a brilliant invention and totally fun. Be forewarned: You can lose a few hours here faster than anywhere else online, but, in the course of so doing, you can discover some otherwise almost impossible-to-find trea-sures. EBay is a great place to find a wedding gown at a dis-count—and what tranny isn't looking for that! Buyers and sellers on eBay report on one another's reliability, so there is a self-policing system that proves quite efficient. I received a beautiful silver compact with a "V" monogram as a gift from friends who are eBay fanatics.

Panty plethora. Even if you have become the most polit-ically correct, conservative tranny, there may still be a soft spot in your heart for ruffled rumba pants, see-through bikinis, satin tap pants—need I go on? In the past it has not been easy to find variety in these items, but now there is no need to get your knick-ers in a twist, for help has arrived. You have the whole world at your manicured fingertips. You can import your lingerie from Lon-don or Paris, have a drawer full of frilly frocks, or at the least a file folder full. Those British queens rule, offering a wealth of frocks for today's sissy (www.sulis.co.uk).

Let yourself grow. What is the personality of your femme-self? That is another very important factor to consider when you choose where to shop. Just who are you shopping for? A sophis-ticated career woman? Mommy's little girl? Young model? Sissy maid? Don't worry about being politically correct. If you won't allow yourself to wear a tutu or tiara just because you feel like it, what's the point of being a tranny? Political correctness can stunt your growth.

It is possible, however, to have too much of a good thing. In order to avoid falling into a frilly fashion rut, you can visit the Land's End site (www.landsend.com); create your virtual model—primitive though she is—and dress her in butch gear just to stay in balance.

Some of you girls are not old enough to wear bras or corsets or garter belts or any of those sexy clothes that big girls wear. If you are a baby tranny—and in this case I mean a big girl in a little dress—I want to offer you the prettiest, frilliest dress I can find. That's what you deserve, sweetheart. Who could understand that better than another tranny? That's who will be designing for you at LD Fashions. The owner, Laura Walton, explains that he was taught to sew by his wife. This is the chance for you Catholic-school trannies to wear the Communion dress that you have yearned for since age seven. You could even relive your christening and give yourself a brand-new name.

The Name Game

Being a tranny is your chance to re-create yourself, and it can be quite helpful to give yourself a new name. What's in a name?

Plenty. If you do not have a name for your femmeself, I encourage you to choose one and encourage you to use your imagination. You can get some help at www.babynames.com. Names have meaning. Many of you ladies in waiting choose names that are the feminization of your male names. Let's see what some of your names mean. We have lots of Stephanies here at the academy. Stephanie means "crown." It is more than the feminine form of Steve. Stephanie is a regal name, a name that encourages you to hold your head high, especially when wearing your prom dress and tiara. All of you Dons who call yourselves Donna are very correct, because Donna means "lady," and I expect you to act like one. You Irish Pats who call yourselves Patricia have also picked a name that means "noblewoman," as in "patrician." And Michelle is the femme version of Michael, as in the angel or godlike one.

Christine also has religious significance and refers to the "anointed one." You are the anointed one each time you adorn yourself with lipstick and lingerie.

You might pick a name because you like the sound of it, or it may remind you of a woman who you admire and would like to emulate. Some of the most popular names of the eighties have been Jessica, Jennifer, Melissa, and Ashley. When I started my school, there were so many Jennifers enrolled that I thought I might call the academy "the school for Jennifers." Jennifers will be happy to know that the name means "fair one." You Jessicas are "women of wealth" and "Melissa" comes from the Greek word that means "honey"—perhaps that's why you are so sweet.

Names can be inspiring. My parents named me Mary, after my own mother, my grandmothers, and, of course, the mother of God. At confirmation I picked Veronica, which means "true image" and was also the name of the rich girl in the *Archie* comic books who got all the boys, especially Archie. Veronica felt more true to the image that I was going for than Mary, the world's most famous virgin.

If you do not yet have a name or are perhaps considering a name change, here are some suggestions. Amanda, one of the most popular names of the late nineties, is more than a great play on words for academy girls. The name means "deserving of great love" and you are. Ashley is a favorite of you Southern belles. It was popularized by the movie *Gone With the Wind*. Ashley is also a name that can be used by both sexes. Plus it is the name of my pussy, our academy mascot, and she is a beauty.

I've always thought Angela, "the heavenly messenger," was a beautiful name. Linda means "pretty." Irish names have a lovely ring. Shannon means "little wise one." Rhiannon, also the title of the classic song by Fleetwood Mac, means "magic maiden." Now isn't that inspiring? Rebecca means "faithful." But if you feel like a hussy you might prefer to call yourself Wanda, the "wanton one." Renée is French for "one who is born again," and Natasha means the same thing in Greek. Here is an interesting Greek name: Cassandra is a confuser of men. If that seems like a mouthful, you can call yourself Sandi or Cassie for short.

If you would like to have a lovely voice, you might choose Carol as a reminder. Chatty Samanthas may be surprised to know that the name means "she who listens." If you love strong women, Astrid means "divine strength and power." Tracy means a fighter. Emily means "hardworking and ambitious," perfect for a sophisticated career woman.

I love simple names like Ann, Grace, and Jane, which mean "blessed," "charming," and "gracious," in that order.

You might choose the name of a famous movie star, like Meg, a form of Margaret, which means "pearl" or "precious one." Cher means "dear one." Julia is "youthful." This is a concept I know appeals to you, besides being the name of the current box-office queen.

Names of places are also fashionable. How about India or Italia? Is there a Holly Wood out there? Warhol superstar Holly Woodlawn took her "walk on the wild side" and inspired Lou Reed (www.hollywoodlawn.com). She named herself after a cemetery and was immortalized. Names that play on words are total fun and follow a grand tranny tradition. Some of my favorite names belong to New York performing artists like Miss Understood, Imperial Court members Traila Trash, Tami Wynotte, and Shonda Lear. Not long ago my student Gayle, who is in her late fifties and until recently has lived a very traditional straight male life, told me she has decided to give herself the middle name Candace. That way, her nickname can be Gay Candy. I considered it a very liberating step on her path to self-discovery. At the website of the movie *Hedwig and the Angry Inch* (www.hedwigmovie.com), you can discover your glam rock name. I'm pleased to say mine is Gilded Crotch.

So the answer to the question What's in a name? is plenty, and I encourage you to make the most of yours. Change it if you like. Give yourself a middle name, a new last name. This is your opportunity to be free; be the girl of your dreams, Desiree.

Oh, baby! As a tranny, you can be not only reborn, you can grow up. Sometimes, the place to start is in a diaper. Many academy students identify as young models or sophisticated career women but there are some who want to be mommy's little girl—and many who would be if given the chance. Let's talk about some of you big little girls.

Size does not matter. You can feel like a toddler inside and still be well over six feet tall, or you may be slim and slight. Charlie was about five foot ten with a strong, muscular chest—like a mattress a girl could bounce up and down on. He had a tough-guy accent and even smoked a cigar. But that stogie was merely a substitute for the nipple from which he was never weaned. He had deliberated for some months after learning of the academy before he contacted us. It takes a big man to admit he wants to be a baby.

Miss Viqui and I supervised Charlie's rebirth as baby Tiffany. I began by sprinkling baby powder all over Charlie and giving him a baby powder massage. A baby powder massage is sheer delight, I promise you. Baby needed her diaper and we just happened to have a few nice, soft, fluffy cloth diapers at the academy. While I diapered baby Tiffany, making sure to add more powder to the area to be diapered so baby would not get diaper rash, Miss Viqui took photographs for baby's first album. We used safety pins with plastic tops to secure Tiffany's diaper. Then we put her in an adorable ruffled romper printed with tiny giraffes and teddy bears. We added a pair of white patent leather Mary Janes (www.mary -janeshoes.com) and pink ankle socks with white lace trim. Then, using beard cover, light makeup, and pigtailed wig, we completed the transformation.

The best part was when I held baby Tiffany in my arms, close to my heart. (Baby Tiffany seemed to enjoy this quite a bit, too.) She rested her head against my breast as I rocked her, not to sleep but surely to dream. At the conclusion of class, Charlie told me this was one time that reality surpassed imagination. I encouraged him to take home the baby powder and leave it near the bed to be handy the next time he and his wife made love. He looked at me like I was totally mad but tucked the container into his briefcase and took a powder.

**Patti and Caprice get ready to be bridesmaids.
(Photo by Nancy Rica Schiff)**

CHAPTER 6

Makeup

ow do you rate your makeup skills? No matter what your relationship with cosmetics, you will find something in this chapter for you. As a boy who wants to be a girl, you are probably fascinated with makeup, the same as most girls, but you may feel totally inept. Don't worry; you can improve. Let's start first in an area that is more familiar to you and very, very important: your beard and how to tame it. Chances are you have not permanently removed your facial hair, so beard cover is essential. That is the one step that you won't find in the great books by the late Kevyn Aucoin (www .kevinaucoin.com) or other makeup artists. But before you cover your beard, you must be clean shaven. I recommend a good barbershop shave. There appears to be nothing better than the male ritual of an old-fashioned barbershop shave to prepare you for your entry into femininity.

Erika's Close Shave

Before his visit to the academy Erika Thomas treated himself to a shave at the Art of Shaving (www.theartofshaving .com), an enterprise devoted to luxurious shaving owned by Eric Malka and Myriam Zaoui, a husband-and-wife team. There are five locations—three in Manhattan, one in Miami, and one in Dallas—staffed by professional barbers who are expertly trained in the fine art of hot-towel shaves. The stores sell shaving necessities and accoutrements. There are no cans of shaving cream for sale, no electric razors. The Classic Shave lasts a good thirty minutes and includes a steaming, hot-towel wrap, facial massage accompanied by a hot lather, very close shave, followed by an alum-block rub and a cold towel wrap to close pores. Finally, aftershave milk is applied to soothe the skin. One satisfied customer said it was as if this was his first shave after having worn a beard all his life. His face felt that smooth. Erika Thomas agreed it was the best shave she ever had and her lovely baby's-bottom complexion proved it. She got extra credit points from Miss Deborah, dean of cosmetology, who has on previous occasions sent many a student off to the washroom to reshave his face.

The proprietors of the Art of Shaving offer products and expert advice at the shops and online. The descriptions of lavender and sandalwood ingredients, lush badger bristle brushes, and creamy soaps sounded so delightful, I almost wanted a beard of my own . . . just kidding. It was the pampering that made it all so inviting. So why not turn your dreaded morning ritual into a sensuous face feast with aromatherapy-inspired products and fine accessories? Or take yourself to your local barber and let him apply that hot towel to soften your beard before he soaps you up and shaves you. You deserve it, princess.

Tips for Bearded Ladies

1. Your face needs to be warm and moist for a shave. So shave in the shower or immediately afterward, never before.
2. Use hot water when you shave because this will open your pores.
3. Do not use shaving foams or gels as these contain numbing agents that stiffen your beard and close your pores. Instead, use a glycerin-based shaving cream or shaving soap.
4. Use a good razor, like the Mach3 from Gillette.
5. Shave in the direction your hairs grow. Then, to get closer, relather your beard and shave again against the grain.
6. Be gentle. Too much pressure on the blade causes razor burn.
7. Finish off with an alcohol-free moisturizer.

These rules apply each time you shave, no matter if you are preparing for femme mode or no. You can change your look many times, but you have only one face.

Model Students

Besides shaving, there are other things that accompany a rough-and-ready male lifestyle that need to be addressed. Drinking is one of them. Alcohol is very hard on the complexion whether you are slapping it on, as in aftershaves or colognes, or knocking 'em down, as in whiskey and rye. I am not telling you to cut out drinking. Moderate drinking is fine, as my quick-tongued porn star girlfriend Gloria Leonard likes to say, "Everything in moderation, including moderation." But if you are going to drink at all, even coffee, drink plenty of water. In fact, always drink plenty of water. Every model will agree. On the streets of New York, models can always be spotted carrying their bottles of Evian inside the net pockets attached to their Prada backpacks. These people are making a living from their faces, and you, my dear, glamour-girl wanna-be, need be no less vigilant. How much water do you need to drink? Most likely, more than you drink at present. Six to eight eight-ounce glasses a day is ideal.

Face It

At Miss Vera's academy we offer complete makeup training with our expert deans. Miss Deborah is the head of the cosmetology department. But not all students want to learn how to do their own makeup. Some prefer to be pampered and "be done." To have your makeup applied by another is a very sensual experience, especially when it is being applied by a beautiful blonde like Miss Deborah, who uses the most delicate strokes to transform you from male to female. But I would like to motivate you to learn to do your own makeup because

a. You can do it!
b. You will feel more confident to go out and going out is fun.
c. You cannot always depend on someone else to do it for you.
d. You can do it!

Brush up. Like any project, from building a house to sewing on a button, it is important to have the right tools. Many students come to the academy with makeup bags bulging with lipsticks, eye shadows, foundations, and powders, but very rarely do these budding debutantes have the right applicator sponges or makeup brushes. Painters know the importance of using the right brush for a particular job or area, and so should you. You will be so pleased at how much easier your makeup is to apply, as if magic has just seeped into you fingers. Well, anyway, there will be a definite improvement in your technique. A list of basic brushes includes:

1. Loose powder: one-inch-wide goat or pony hair, domed or round.
2. Blush: three-quarter-inch wide goat or pony hair, domed, angled, or round.
3. Lip: sable.
4. Eye shadow brushes:
   a. across the eyelid: ½" use for lighter colors.
   b. at the crease: ¼" slanted brush.
   c. outer corners: use a pointed or Q-tip-shaped brush and darker colors.
   d. overall blending: ½", a bit firmer than the eyelid brush.
5. Eyeliner (the slimmer the brush, the more control).

Goat hair brushes tend to hold the product better, while pony-hair brushes can be softer. Domed brushes offer more control, and angled brushes can help you achieve more drama. For your first brushes, I recommend a domed powder brush and round blush brush. Sable is the softest, which is what you want around your delicate eyes. You can start off with just an eyelid brush for shadow and then expand later, as you develop more skill. Be sure to look for brushes that carry the assurance that no animals have been harmed. After you dip your brush in any powder makeup always tap the brush before you apply the color. Makeup is much easier to add than subtract.

We are putting together our own line of brushes for academy students, and I invite you to visit our website to find out more. I also recommend brushes by MAC (www.maccosmetics.com), where you will find an inventory to make your pretty head spin. At MAC retail shops, the artists will help you sort through your confusion. Makeup Mania (www.makeupmania.com) and Spa Cadet (www.spacadet.com) have names and product lines, including brushes, that are right up your alley. You don't need to spend a fortune on brushes, but good brushes are important. So if it is a choice between buying yet another lipstick when you already have a bunch or putting your pretty pennies toward a lipstick brush, choose the brush.

Tranny Beauty Basics

There is considerable information in my first book about makeup application. In this book I would like to reemphasize the things that are still most important and guide you to places where you can find additional inspiration. Makeup really is an art, and I would like you to be exposed to the many artists in the field. The look that Miss Deborah creates most often at the academy we refer to as "Miss Real." Our girls are not stage performers. They are ladies who lunch. But even in our daytime look, we do more than a girl who was not born with your challenges would do. These extras include:

1. Beard cover
2. False eyelashes
3. Groomed eyebrows
4. Wig

For beard cover, use Ben Nye's 5 O'Clock Sharp or Joe Blasco Blue Neutralizer #2. We order these by the caseload from our 19th Street neighbor Alcon NYC, and you can find them at other good makeup supply houses. Makeup artist Jim Bridges (www.jbridges.com), a name well known in the tranny community, includes beard cover in his line of products. (A bit of gossip: Joe has many celebrity clients—such as Joan Collins, Farrah Fawcett, and Sophia Loren—but Jim also lent his talents to the adult film industry and was the makeup artist on the set of *Consenting Adults,* the very first X-rated movie in which I appeared. So when I first met Jim it was all about taking clothes off, and now we are both in the business of putting clothes on.) Joey V., aka Toy Girl, the resident artist at Pat Field's Hotel Venus, tackles a stubborn beard by applying foundation with an airbrush. To avoid that overly powdered look, after you have given yourself a dusting of finishing powder, take a damp makup sponge and pat your face with it—you'll be all dewey and fresh. Where there's a makeup artist, there's a way!

False eyelashes are the most challenging to apply, but they make a big difference in your appearance and are worth the effort. We use them for both day and night. I recommend you start off with demi-lashes. These are a bit shorter than full lashes and easier for you to manipulate. Apply eyelash glue to the base of one strip of eyelashes, then use tweezers to lift the strip to your eyelid. Position the lash strip as close to the edge of your eyelid as possible. Be sure to place the strip on your skin, not on your own lashes. You don't want to lose your precious real lashes when you remove the faux ones. Use the blunt end of a clean orange stick to tap down the strip. (Note: An orange stick does not mean an orange slice. An orange stick is a little wooden stick that is used most often in manicures. Can anyone tell me how the orange stick got its name?)

Once you have mastered the art of false eyelashes, you can move on to eyelash bindis, strips of diamonds for your eyelids that I think every girl needs (www.adiscountbeauty.com).

Eyebrows are an area in which less is not always better. How many times have you seen a person who has shaved off her own brows and replaced them with thin lines. Fashion is fickle. Believe it or not, women in the seventeenth century used false eyebrows made from mouse hides to give themselves a look of perpetual surprise. This and other more useful tips and styles are found in *The Eyebrow,* a book by Robyn Casio. Your eyebrows can go a long way to making your face not only more feminine but also more intriguing and glamorous. You will, most likely, need to begin by cleaning up your natural brow. You can do this with tweezers or you can remove those straggly hairs permanently by electrolysis. Electrolysis is definitely worth serious consideration here—especially for those hairs that, no matter what your fashion statement, definitely need to go. Another method of removal, popular with East Indian women, is "threading," in which eyebrows are removed with thread. This method is not permanent; it lasts quite a bit longer than waxing, but it is more painful. It is not expensive.

If you are not sure what style brow you would like or which would look good on you, or you feel all thumbs when it comes to actually drawing it in, there is help at Eyebrowz (www .eyebrowz.com). They offer over eighty stencils that imitate the brows of famous beauties like Liz Taylor, Cindy Crawford, and many, many more. You can also buy the powders and brushes to make the brows happen.

Makeup Mentors

Behind every great queen there is a great makeup artist. That artist could be you, but if it is not, then you better make sure you have someone else in mind for the job. A makeup artist makes a great friend. She knows that there is no catastrophe so irreparable that it cannot be improved by a good layer of paint. I find that I get more work done when I brighten my face with a little lippy. You will be happy to know that our academy plans include the opportunity to enroll for online consultations and even transformations with our cosmetology deans. You can find lots of useful information in makeup books by Kevyn Aucoin, Bobbi Brown, and other artists. At the Joe Blasco site (www.joeblasco.com), there are illustrated step-by-step instructions. A real treat is porn star Asia Carrera's site (www.asiacarrera.com), where you are offered Asia's makeup routine and colorful commentary. With all this information available to you, there is no need for me to go through each step. I think it is more important for you to learn as much as you can about makeup from as many people as you can, then mix it all together in your own style.

Makeup is color, and color is meant to be played with. It is a tool and a toy. There are no real rules about how you should look. There are some expectations. For instance, high-contrast makeup looks better in the evening than the daytime. Daytime calls for more natural and muted tones. Basic rules of art apply, e.g., what is light stands out, what is dark recedes. But other than that, you are free to experiment.

Lipstick Rules

If you don't have much time for makeup, then just go with one thing, lipstick. There is *always* time for lipstick. Once when I was asked how America might be made a better place, I put my faith in lipstick.

You might think that as dean of the world's first male-to-female cross-dressing academy, I would recommend that America could be better if each man cross-dressed or learned at least to walk a mile in a woman's high heels. I do admit that those thoughts crossed my mind, but in some situations, less is more. In this one, I recognized that a little lipstick would go a long, long way.

I suggest that every man wear lipstick for a week—bright red, blue-pink, even tangerine lipstick, no neutral or translucent shades. I thought about this as I walked to the gym one morning. I imagined my doorman's crimson lips upturned in a bright smile of greeting. The homeless man lying on the street would look less scary, less disgusting, and more approachable. He would be more like a girl who has partied all night and gone to sleep with her makeup on.

The butchers and fish sellers, dressed in their white coats in the market, would look up from their work, all sexy and red lipped, almost ready to burst into song. The businessmen hustling to their jobs would seem alert and excited and turned on to the day. Lipstick makes men gay, as in happy. It throws you off-kilter. You do not know what to expect, and others do not know what to expect from you—nor you from yourself. You would feel a little foolish and that would be very liberating. Lipstick adds color to life. It could free men from the bondage of their male egos. That bloodred mouth exposes the yellow bellies you so desperately hide, your vulnerabilities. Of course, it also lays open your vanities and accentuates your hunger—and, believe me, I am in a position to know.

If every man were required to wear lipstick for a week, there would be a lot less fighting and a lot more kissing. Theater would happen in the streets. Life could be more like a Broadway musical. And the lessons of that week would be remembered, for the lipstick would leave an indelible mark. Men have been taught to use their fists and reach for a gun. Women have always been the shrewder sex; our weapons are more subtle. With a tiny lipstick tube, we get ready, take aim, and fire—and with it we can change the world.

Student Jennifer Summers (Photo by Mariette Pathy Allen)

CHAPTER 7

Let Down Your Hair

apunzel, Rapunzel, let down your hair! Do you remember that lovely fairy tale? Perhaps as a boy you may not have learned it, or you may need a refresher. You can find the whole story in a book of Grimm's fairy tales. Briefly, Rapunzel is a beautiful girl who, because of the transgressions of her parents, was locked away in a room at the top of a high tower for many years by a wicked witch. Rapunzel had beautiful long golden hair and it was by calling, "Rapunzel, Rapunzel, let down your hair" and using her long golden hair as a ladder that a handsome young prince discovered Rapunzel and the two fell in love. Of course, there were other trials and tribulations, but eventually Rapunzel and the prince lived happily ever after. Fairy tales have deep psychological significance, and Rapunzel is no exception. In the case of this story, think of yourself as both Rapunzel and the prince. Your hair is one way that your male persona discovers your beautiful femmeself and rescues her from oblivion. There are many ways, my dear Rapunzel, that you can in the most tangible sense let down your hair.

The easiest method is to let your natural hair grow, but that is not always possible. For one thing, you may be bald. For another, you may feel the need to maintain a close-cropped appearance at least part of the time. Another consideration is that your own hair may not do the trick in providing the most flattering frame for your femme face.

Fairy Tales Can Come True

Here is what happened when Pamela Peters came to visit.

Prior to his arrival, Peter e-mailed me several photos of himself and what he described as his "long hair." For Peter, it may have seemed long—he was used to years in a buzz cut—but in reality his hair was only a few inches long, nowhere near long enough for our purposes at the academy. Peter seemed to want to use his own hair as is and effect a kind of man-in-a-dress look. I am not against that and think we all need to be free to wear whatever we like. But there was another consideration. Peter was coming to me for educational purposes. He had never seen himself totally transformed, and I believed that he could learn more if, when he looked in the mirror, he saw as soft and pretty a reflection of his femmeself, Pamela, as possible. This would give him more options. If he wanted to effect some combination later, that would be fine. So I advised him to allow Pamela to wear a wig.

From the size of Peter's face in the photographs, I knew that Pamela would need a lot more hair. The size and shape of your face determine which hairstyle is most flattering. In Peter's case, his face was big and square. Peter as Pamela would look very pretty with hair at least shoulder length and in a style with a bit of height to elongate her face. This was a job for Shannon, wig stylist extraordinaire.

I logged onto Shannon's Wigtech N.Y.C. site (www.wigtech.com) and immediately saw a wig I thought would be perfect. Then I called Shannon and asked if she could drop by to pick up some of our academy 'do's for restyling and to discuss a new student.

Shannon is a lovely tranny with an alabaster complexion, big blue eyes, and long raven curls, not unlike what our student Pamela would love to have if she grew her locks many more inches. Over tea, we gossiped about Shannon's days at Pat Field's Eighth Street salon where she did color, styling, cuts—the whole kit and kaboodle in the "salon without limits." "The woman knew how to make you work," she said, referring to Ms. Field. Up until its close, Shannon was in charge of the wig department at the late and great Lee Brewster's Mardi Gras Boutique. Shannon's earned her golden teasing comb.

I showed her the photograph of Peter soon-to-be Pamela and Shannon agreed with my selection. When I told her that Peter would also love to use his own hair, Shannon said she would bring an assortment of wigs and pieces for our girl to play with.

The class was a hair happening. Miss Deborah used her paints, powders, and lots of patience to transform Peter, who was quite animated and chatty during the makeup application. Some students are quiet as mice until their transformation is complete and then they become extroverts. Others are nervous and hyperactive at the start, then peaceful and calm once they see their femme-selves. Whether Peter or Pamela, this student was a chatterbox, but there was one moment of quiet.

Shannon arrived with bags and boxes of wigs. She put the first wig on Pamela's head. Pamela/Peter looked in the mirror and was stunned into silence. Her face softened into a big smile. She wrapped her arms around herself and felt the silk of her negligee, then shifted her weight to one leg. She nearly melted. Then she thrust her pelvis forward, reached her hands up, lifted her hair off her neck, and piled it atop her head, feeling the sexpot within. She stared unbelievingly into the mirror, then turned to show herself to us and have us confirm what she almost could not believe with her own big, blue eyes. Pamela was beautiful.

"You look like Kirstie Alley," we all exclaimed. Pamela beamed.

"That wig is a monofilament," said Shannon. Monofilament refers to the material from which the wig is made. A monofilament wig has the most real-looking scalp because the hairs are sewn into a clear material that lets the wearer's own scalp show through. A detailed explanation of monofilament wigs is offered at www.wigsalon.com.

Another very realistic wig is one with a lace cap. The lace cap presents the most versatile and natural hairline. The lace actually comes down over the wearer's forehead and is cut to fit, then glued at the edge. With a lace cap base, a girl can have a widow's peak, a V-shaped hairline. In the forties the widow's peak was considered such a flattering hairline that Hollywood starlets were shipped off to stylists immediately upon signing contracts to have their hairlines reshaped.

Shannon continued to tantalize Pamela with tresses and treats. She tossed a headband to Pamela and told her to take off the wig and put the headband over her head and around her neck. Then Shannon fastened hairpieces—long full curly ones, long shiny straight ones, even one that reversed from a blunt cut on one side to a layered cut on the other. After each piece was fastened, the headband was pulled up. In this way, Pamela's own hair was used from forehead to headband and the faux tresses cascaded down her back. Since Pamela was a broad-shouldered, big-boned girl, Shannon brought lots of long hair. With each wig, each piece, and each color, our girl's appearance changed. Black hair was a harder look. She turned her into Mistress Pamela, a zaftig dominatrix. With the long blunt cut, she was good little Pammy, an Alice in Wonderland.

Framing Your Face

Wearing a wig is fun. You don't have to abide by any style rules, especially if you are not planning to go out. Love is blind. It is amazing the design flaws your mind's eye can overlook when you gaze in the mirror. But if you want your wig to complement your face to the utmost, there are some definite ways to accomplish this. Take a look in the mirror. Is your face oval? (Your forehead is slightly wider than your chin.) Square? (You have a square hairline and a square chin.) Round? (Your hairline and your chin are round.) Oblong? (Your face is long and narrow.) Or diamond shaped? (You have wide cheekbones, narrow forehead, and narrow chin.) The general rule has been to choose a hairdo that fills in the areas of your face only where you need it and not where you don't, the goal being an overall, balanced oval shape.

A square face needs a side part and some height at the top. A round face also needs height at the top, but a center part. Oblong-faced girls can wear bangs and have fullness at the top. A diamond face needs hair swept away from the ears (the widest part of the diamond) but added to the top at the temples and jawline where the face is most narrow. An oval face is most versatile, but there are other considerations for you.

I have found that boys who want to be girls are often helped by soft curls. This is especially true if you dream of wearing a French braid, French twist, Grecian curls, or any updo. Lots of falling tendrils help soften the look. We have one wig that looks good on almost everyone. It is called Vogue by Rene Margu, but other manufacturers make a similar style. It is a short, full, curly do that lifts the face and fills it out, though on a big, round head, the effect is clownish and definitely a hair don't. A thick neck can use longer hair to make it less noticeable. But hair that is too long and not cut to frame the face gives that George-of-the-Jungle look, another miss-take.

An indispensable tool in our academy wig class is the Polaroid camera. We photograph you in each wig that we try, then use the snapshots to help us decide which looks best. Occasionally, there is a wig that is not worth a photo, but blink and you might miss it, because if we decide it's best not remembered, we rip it off quick.

Hair Care

Caring for your wig can be very simple. Some wigs just need a shampoo and will dry right back into shape. One of the considerations Pamela had in choosing her wig was maintenance. She wanted something she would be able to take care of on her own. At Wigtech, Shannon lists lots of helpful hair hints. Among them:

To wash wig

1. Brush wig thoroughly, starting at ends and working up to the cap.
2. Add mild shampoo to cool water in either basin or sink.
3. Immerse wig and swish gently.
4. Soak for five minutes.

5. Rinse thoroughly in cool, clear water until all soap is removed.
6. You may use any over-the-counter hair conditioner (preferably one with lanolin) to condition your wig.
7. Work the conditioner in well from cap to ends. Leave it in for five minutes, then rinse thoroughly.
8. Squeeze wig gently and blot it with a towel.
9. Place wig over wig form or tall slender object (like a tall hair-spray can) and let wig dry naturally.
10. Brush wig gently only when it's completely dry.
11. You may now restyle your wig.

Caution: Do not expose your wig to open flame or excessive heat. Do not use heat appliances such as curling irons or hair dryers on your wig.

You may use conventional rollers or hot rollers on a medium heat setting to reset your wig.

If you do not feel confident to restyle your own wig, you can pay a stylist to do it. Some beauty salons offer this service. Most wig salons offer a styling service on wigs that you have purchased from them. They might charge extra if you have purchased your wig elsewhere. And if your wig is really in bad shape—the color has faded or your crowning glory looks more like roadkill—you may have to bury her and buy a new one.

Wigstock Remembered

Let's take a moment to remember Wigstock (www .wigstock.nu), that happy hair-o-ween party that took place annually in Manhattan each Labor Day weekend. Wigstock grew out of the bewigged brains of the "Lady" Bunny and friends seventeen years ago when they were all very, very young and performing at the Pyramid Club in the East Village. The first Wigstock took place at Tompkins Square Park and continued there for many years, then became such a big girl she had to find a new home, which she did after much political wrangling, at the piers in the West Village.

Everyone wore wigs to Wigstock, the wilder the better. There was always a strong puppy dog contingent. Over the years, the town's most talented home-grown and visiting trannies performed there: RuPaul, John Cameron (*Hedwig*) Mitchell, John Kelly as Joni Mitchell, Mistress Formika, Joey Arias, Candis Cayne, Kiki & Herb . . . and more, as well as music stars Deborah Harry, the B-52s and others who are happily honorary trannies. Our academy girls enjoyed great adventures there. I even sent three students to Wigstock on assignment from the school of high-heel journalism. Jennifer James brought home the story, Stephanie womaned the camera, and Susan Sergeant stood in the background with her mouth open, she was so amazed. The power of Wigstock was in its ability to spread fun and a sense of community as thick as Dippity-Do across the city. At the same time, Wigstock was all about freedom.

After seventeen years the "Lady" Bunny and the other organizers decided "this troubled teen has become too much of a handful." Lady Bunny is pursuing a music career and says she'll "happily trade sexual favors for a recording contract." Thank goodness, there is *Wigstock,* the movie, a reminder to us all of what heights can be reached with a lotta love and a lotta hair.

Patti Gets the Brush Off

Here is a cautionary tale of hair care. When Patricia Harrington began to take hormones for her transition from male to female, she was elated. But this feeling did not compare with the euphoria she experienced when she got her new hair. She purchased it from Angelo David, Int'l, N.Y.C. It is actually a human hair system, glued in place, worn 24/7 and removed only once a week when she shampoos it. Patti went from a semibald man with a frizzy St. Francis to an amber-haired colleen with swinging Joni Mitchell tresses. She is now an academy graduate and has become my good girlfriend. Each Friday while I worked on this book, Patti and I got together for dinner and conversation. Before we left my apartment she would stand in front of the mirror and gently brush her hair. She loved brushing her hair. One day, she did it quite absentmindedly while we chatted. Unfortunately she was using a slim, round plastic-bristled brush from Vidal Sassoon. Before either of us realized it, the brush was stuck, strands of hair twisted around it. We each tried to untangle it, making little progress. I knew Patti's hair had cost her hundreds of dollars and she was very proud of it. I worried that she might panic or get angry or even start crying. But after twenty minutes, she still remained cool.

"Maybe we could slide a screwdriver or something under the hair to help loosen it," Patti, who is quite the handywoman, suggested.

I went to my tool drawer and pulled out the first likely item, a needle-nosed jewelry pliers, and worked it under her hair. What was this? Now the pliers as well as the cheap plastic brush was stuck in her hair. I had to hold back my laughter as I envisioned Patti walking down the street with a head full of hardware. The miracle was, the old Pat would have been a wreck, while Patricia was cool, calm, and collected. Eventually, our manipulations with the pliers worked. Patti was released. The round brush immediately went into the garbage. I advise you girls to avoid this particular tool. Plastic brushes in general are not good for your hair, whether it be faux or real. Boar bristle brushes are the best for real hair and metal brushes for fake. A round brush, especially a tiny one, requires more skill than a conventional brush. The lessons I want you to remember from this story are: 1) When it comes to your hair, plastic is not fantastic. 2) When using a round brush, keep your mind on your head.

A Tiara in Every Pot

Now that we have chosen the right hairdo, I think you need a tiara to go with it. Tiaras evoke thoughts of brides and beauty pageants, debutantes and prom queens. Delta Burke, who won many a beauty pageant, admitted the hardest thing to give up at the end of a reign was her tiara. Once you own one, you will never be the same. The very best tiaras I have seen were designed by the jewelers of the Imperial Court of New York, Robert Sorrell, Larry Vrba, and David Mandell (www.imperialcourtny.org). The first time I saw these creations it was like watching Chrysler Buildings float through the ballroom. Ron's Rhinestones (www .ronsrhinestones.com), offers a huge selection of tiaras and even a total diamanté dress, if you want to spread the wealth across your derrière. You can also shop for tiaras at Ejools (www.ejools.com). Every queen needs a crown, and you are no exception.

I once owned a very special tiara, designed by Larry Vrba, and it was regal and sparkly. But what endeared it to me was that it was a gift from Lee Brewster, the owner of Lee's Mardi Gras Boutique. One day, I sent it uptown in a taxi along with one of the deans and a student. They were on their way to a photo shoot at the studio of our dean of photography, Mariette Pathy Allen. The tiara was in a colorful cotton shoulder sack along with a purple boa. I tossed the sack into the taxi at the last moment thinking that the items would make great photo props. Unfortunately, I did not give anyone specific instructions to be in charge of the sack, and it got left behind in the taxi. Somewhere in this city, a person stepped into a taxi and found that tiara and boa. I wonder who? I don't doubt that the items found a good home. A tiara and boa could make even a bad home good.

**Student Michelle Williams on a
"Bite of the Big Apple" tour
(Photo by Miss Vera)**

CHAPTER 8

Arts & Entertainment

ew York, like major cities here and abroad, hosts many venues where boys who want to be girls can be entertained, be the entertainment, or both. Let me take you on a guided tour. At the academy, we have named this "A Bite of the Apple," and you will be tonight's "Eve." Accompanying us will be Miss Melissa, our dean of etiquette, who will make sure you keep your purse in your lap and pay heed to other such details, and Miss Topaz, who will pay close attention to your hair and makeup so that you don't get too rumpled. Both deans are wonderful conversationalists and will pry you out of your shell and polish you to a pearly luster. I have the utmost confidence in the deans, and I know you are in good hands. Tonight I will be along, of course, so that I can report on this field trip.

A girl's got to eat—even if you are squeezed into that tight-fitting corset. It will be hard to resist the meals at Lips (www
.lipsnyc.com), the drag restaurant that we visit so often it has
been called our academy halfway house. Lips is sort of the Hard
Rock Café of drag, a theme restaurant, but without a manufactured
feel. It's just a few blocks from the academy, so we can walk there.
Yes, dear, you can feel the wind up your skirt, perhaps for the very
first time. So, besides being a bit nervous—or as I prefer to say,
excited—you may feel a chill in areas you never experienced. The
restaurant's entrance is discreet. The only thing in the window is a
red neon sculpture of lips with the name in the center. As soon as
we walk through the door, you will be hit with a riot of color and
lots of gold—lamé and otherwise. The décor is over-the-top opu-
lence. The first time I saw the interior, I was reminded of Harrie's,
a gay bar that I once visited in Bangkok. It, too, was gold from
floor to ceiling and filled with gilt pineapples. At Lips, the décor is
dominated by jewels, huge jewels in deep ruby red, emerald green,
sapphire blue. The glitter and jewels seem to pulse with the music.
And you, my dear girl, are mesmerized.

We are warmly greeted by Coco LaChine, our glamorous and
gracious hostess. Coco's wearing a slinky, sequined, dragon-red
cocktail dress that shows off her elegant figure, and a big blond
updo. "Good evening, Miss Vera," she says. "So nice to see all of
you." Air kisses all around. And I introduce you, our happy debutante. "Congratulations," says Miss Coco. She totally appreciates
your bravery. She also inspects your outfit. "That dress is very becoming." It's a black lace sheath with a deep sweetheart neckline,
and the skirt accentuates your curvy bottom.

Once at the table, you relax a bit and take a good look around.
All over the walls there are pictures of New York's most famous
and popular drag performers (www.queenmother.tv/nycgirl.html):
RuPaul, the "Lady" Bunny, Miss Coco herself in her role as Empress

of the Imperial Court of New York, Joey Arias, Sherry Vine, and so many more. There are costumes as well: pink toe shoes from Les Ballets Trocadero, wigs worn at Wigstock, a tiara from *To Wong Foo*. At the bar, Frankie Cocktail, who is best described as Dolly Parton on steroids, uses his muscled arms to shake a martini over his mountainous breasts. There's nothing subtle about Frankie.

Time to order, sweetheart. You may be too excited to eat, but the deans and I are famished. I think you will find the menu very inspiring. Would you like the Candis Cayne pork chops . . . the Hedda Lettuce organic green salad . . . the Lypsinka shrimp cocktail? The names will be familiar to you, perhaps because they are New York's drag royalty but also because you have been practicing ordering from this menu in the voice class you had with Miss Judy earlier in the day. Now it is your turn to speak up because our fab drag waitress Rajene, who tonight wears a derby with a bright red wig, a multitiered ruffled skirt, and lots of bangle bracelets, is waiting to take your order. She wants to place it with the kitchen before the start of the show and her Cyndi Lauper performance. Miss Topaz leans over solicitously. "Do you know what you would like?" Miss Melissa, with an eye to the challenge presented by your long press-on nails, offers, "I would steer clear of things like linguini." You opt for the Raven-O soup du jour and the Chicklet crab cakes, both single-utensil items. We decide a bottle of Chardonnay will be a nice accompaniment, and the wine arrives right at showtime.

Out come the Lips ladies for a lip-synching extravaganza. Jennifer's doing a Latin number with plenty of twirls, her favorite dance move. Rajene as Cyndi Lauper skips from table to table, draping her long arms and legs across the good-looking men. Petite Gigi with the perky breasts wears a sixties' shift and sings "Xanadu." Gusty Winds, a big mama, is tonight's mistress of ceremonies. She sashays over to the bachelorette party at one end of the room and inspects the bride-to-be's bauble. "Boy, does he love *you*!" she says, very impressed. "What does he do?"

"He's a jeweler."

Now she's really impressed. "Let's give her a very big hand!"

"Any more birthdays?" We've already celebrated a few with cake, candles, crowns, and Polaroid photos. Gusty Winds is headed our way.

"Who else is celebrating something?" I shoot my manicured hand in the air.

"Ah, it's Miss Vera and her class. What's the occasion?" The deans encourage you to stand, the spotlight falls on you, and you just know you are the prettiest girl in the room.

I announce, "First time out!" Trying to remember Miss Judy's instructions, in your best uplifted femme voice you give your name and are greeted by a roomful of cheers. Whew, you did it. You sit down to catch your breath and your smile glows from ear-ring to earring.

Just before we leave, Miss Topaz has you remove your compact from your purse as we all repair our lipstick. And we're off club hopping.

It's still early. Let's bring out the lesbian in you and stop in for a game of pool at Crazy Nanny's (careful not to give away any secrets when you bend over that table in your miniskirt) or listen to the chanteuse in the upstairs lounge at Rubyfruit. Maybe you'd like to go there for dinner sometime.

Miss Melissa is the first with her hand in the air to flag a taxi. Now, we've got to move quickly to make it to Trannie Chasers Night at Nowbar by 11 P.M. Hostess Glorya Wholesome, who proudly proclaims herself New York's only transsexual party promoter (www.glowgirl.com), has invited us to be on her cable TV show, which she hosts each Thursday from Trannie Chasers. The venue is named for tranny admirers, those who want to be with (and sometimes to be) girls with something extra. Glorya is a beautiful platinum blonde with a flawless complexion. She's wearing a glittery silver metallic gown tonight. "Don't worry. My husband, Gil T. Pleasure, will flood the studio with light. We'll all be gorgeous." You, the neophyte, remember her advice and make it part of your tranny credo: big eyes, big lips, big hair, great lighting.

Glorya conducts a very smart and sprightly interview with me and the deans. Since it's your first time out, you're a bit shy and decline. "How about just showing off your pretty self without doing any talking?" says Miss Topaz. "We're very proud of the way you look, you know."

I make you an offer no tranny can refuse: "We'll just have Gil aim the camera at your sexy legs and high heels. You just cross and uncross them a few times so all of New York can ogle." No problem. It's the role you were born to play.

It's 12:30 and the midnight show is just about to start. Allowing for drag time, a half hour late is right on schedule—even a bit early. It's the night of the "Living Legends." The divas are sensational, and so is the audience. Scattered around the bar, some of the club's regular party girls are chatting up potential dates. A well-built fellow in his forties who wears a brown leather jacket offers to buy you a drink. You've been well coached by Miss Eva in what to do in Flirting Fundamentals. "If you are interested enough to chat, accept the drink. But sip it slowly while you get to know him a little. If you don't learn enough to stay interested, don't keep letting him buy you drinks. If you think you could be interested, but not tonight, make it clear during the first drink that you have other plans for the rest of the evening, but play with the straw in your mouth so he knows you are sincere. Then you can exchange contact information for another night. Or gracefully decline another rendezvous with a good reason: you're leaving town . . . your wife would kill you . . . something convincing."

You accept the drink and we notice as he pushes the money toward the barmaid that your lothario has very large hands. Hmmm, could be interesting. He's a longshoreman, how appropriate, because this is your maiden voyage. He's been here before and is quite aware that you are a girl with something extra; in fact, he thinks we all are. Well, it could be the start of a fine romance, but the deans and I whisk you away. Our tour is far from over.

Do you think you can walk three blocks in those three-inch heels? That's the distance to Bar d'O, where we'll catch Joey Arias channeling Billie Holiday. Sherry Vine, just back from performing in Germany, is supposed to make an appearance with Joey. These talented drag queens have become globe-trotting divas of international renown. The crowd at Bar d'O is younger and cooler, not as "on the make" as at Trannie Chasers or at that uptown disco den of decadence, Edelweiss. Speaking of Edelweiss, since it is open this week and not subject to yet another violation and closure, let's hustle up there and treat you to maximum exposure. There are no bachelorette parties at Edelweiss, no birthday cakes or burning candles. But there is plenty of heat. Even the parking lot can be full of action. The club is a lot bigger than the Nowbar, which means more room for trannies and chasers. There are two levels with a dance floor on each level, back staircases, lots of nooks and crannies, and a back room where you can get to know an admirer a bit more intimately. Don't worry, I promise we won't let anyone steal you away, unless you'd like to be.

Maybe you are hungry for adventure, not in the back room, but up on the stage. What does it take to be a tranny star? For one thing, you have to love the limelight and, in most cases, you have to stay up late. Tranny entertainers have spent a lot of time in nightclubs and saloons. Those used to be the only exhibition spaces in town. Our current tour includes many places. We didn't get to them all tonight. There was a time, not very long ago in the sixties and seventies, when trannies did not have so many nightlife options. But as my friend Taxi says, "Thank god for the Gilded Grape." She practically grew up there.

Taxi's Tale

As Taxi tells it, she always felt like a little girl. "I was known as the little queen of the neighborhood. I was always flamboyant and would walk down the street in high heels." Her family was "nice," but she wanted to be "independent." So, at fifteen, she left Richmond and ran away to New York. She moved into the Embassy Hotel on 72nd Street. "I used to call it the punk palace. It was home to just about every queen in New York, young and old." She also started taking hormones that she got from a man named Jimmy Treetops. "He was a white man, real tall, tall, tall. He made the rounds to each floor of the Embassy Hotel like the Avon lady. All those girls knew he was comin' and they had their money ready."

Jimmy Treetops was known in the clubs as a photographer. "He had pictures of every queen in New York, dating back to Holly Woodlawn. He had pictures of me with Grace Jones."

When Taxi arrived in New York she depended on the streets to earn a living. She was a naïve young thing. "I thought everybody was sweet, but I was taken advantage of." Until she found "The Gilded Grape . . . (thank god) . . . my savior.

"At the Gilded Grape bar, I got into shows. On Monday, they had talent shows and I started winning. On Wednesdays, they had go-go boys; and on Sunday, there was a theme show every week, a movie, like *Guess Who's Coming to Dinner*. Everyone who won the talent contests was in the plays. We had to go early on Saturday or Sunday and rehearse. Timmy Scott was the director and he was a genius. People would come from miles around to see these plays and then at eleven, they would have the finale. They served free food every night at 7 P.M., so you know I was down there early. They had hamburgers and french fries. It was like a family.

Taxi recalls, "I played once with Ruby Rims. She was my sister and it was called *Whores & Hookers,* a musical. They were all musicals. Timmy played one of my johns. The john thought I was too innocent to be on the street and that I should be a model and go to Paris. Meanwhile, in the story Ruby's pimp had beaten her up and knocked her on the ground and she was dead. I came with my suitcase in my hand, all ready to leave for Paris, and found my sister dead on the street. I threw the suitcase (I just know it hit somebody upside the head) and fell to the ground sobbing, 'My sister, my sister!' I got a standing ovation. That show made me a star, and got me offa that scared trip."

After years of being on the go, Miss Taxi finally slowed down. Last I heard, she had found a good man and parked herself in the suburbs, where she lives happily.

The bars have a history, as do the queens who gave them life. Some, like the queens who fought back at a bar called the Stonewall and kicked off the Gay Pride movement, helped change our world a lot. Each of them changed the world a little, and so do you.

Life Is Art

Do you aspire to a career in the arts? I have told you that life is art, but perhaps you would like to make a more formal presentation of your art to yourself and to the world. I am not surprised. Many times, particularly during makeup class, I have seen the flame of art rekindled in a student's eyes. "I used to draw," our girl will say, or, "I always wanted to be a fashion designer." But somehow life got in the way. Well, you are not alone. Trannies have infiltrated the arts, going far beyond lip-synching. Not content to be simply the subject of other people's movies, trannies are making their own. The Tranny Fest film festival (www.trannyfest.com) in San Francisco, which was founded by tranny Al Austin and Christopher Lee, is now in its sixth year. Recently the first conference devoted entirely to tranny visual art took place in Troy, New York, at the Fulton Street Gallery. The need for trannies in the performing arts has never waned and is now stronger and more varied than ever. Eddie Izzard (www.izzard.com), the comedian, actor, and social commentator, makes the most of platform pumps, nail varnish, and a bit of lippy, and his appeal is as a sexy tranny who likes girls. Tim Curry in *The Rocky Horror Picture Show* (www .rockyhorror.com) as Dr. Frank-N-Furter changed the lives of many a kid, especially those from the boonies. How you gonna keep 'em down on the farm, after they've seen *Rocky Horror* or become a part of it themselves? You can work as a male actor and still have a bevy of sassy dames in your repertoire like John Leguizamo, or work as a male actor and put all your eggs in one basket like the amazing RuPaul (www.rupaul.com) or the beloved Dame Edna Everage, created by actor Barry Humphries. You can work only in drag and be an actress like Sherry Vine (www.sherryvine.com) or Candis Cayne or a comedienne like Hedda Lettuce (www.hedda.com) or Varla Jean Merman (www.varlaonline.com), or you can work mostly in drag like singer Joey Arias. All but Dame Edna got their start in New York and are now in demand abroad. Why stop at actress? You can write your own shows and be your own star like John Epperson, who is Lypsinka, or Everett Quinton and the late Charles Ludlam, who founded the Ridiculous Theatre Company, or, like Charles Bush, you can make your bones as a tranny off-Broadway and then let your light shine as a Broadway playwright in a non-tranny hit, *The Tale of the Allergist's Wife.*

You might even score a gig as a spokesmodel like RuPaul did for MAC Cosmetics: Ru is an icon, a brilliant wit, an actress, and an actor. Is there any brewery ad campaign that has not included a man in a dress?

Miss Understood is an enterprising tranny. A performance artist herself, she recognized the demand for trannies as everything from headliners to party props and organized the Screaming Queens Entertainment (www.screamingqueens.com). If you know that you want to show off, but you are not sure where your talents lie, you might let Screaming Queens hire you out as a human dessert table, a popular treat at bat mitzvahs.

Tranny artists are famous around the world. Female impersonator Frank Marino (www.frankmarino.com), the star of Las Vegas, boasts that he earns more than the president (and has a much better wardrobe).

The iconoclasm of rock and roll nurtures the tranny spirit. Boy George (www.boy.george.net), Marilyn Manson, and John Cameron "Hedwig and the Angry Inch" Mitchell are among those who have found sanctuary in the rock star ranks. Jayne County proclaims she is "man enough to be a woman." How about you?

Gayle, the blushing bride, and Miss Melissa
(Photo by Mariette Pathy Allen)

CHAPTER 9

Brides "R" Us

*W*ithin days of each other two e-mails were received by our webhostess. One was from a gentleman who was eager to be a bride inquiring about our services and another was from a person who had a wedding gown for sale. The seller described the gown as queen size and said it had been made for a two-hundred-pound bride who was five foot seven and a size 18. I wondered just what was meant by "queen size." Most of our queens are a bit taller. Was the seller a tranny? I didn't know. The signature "Shelly" offered no clue. Neither message surprised me, since the bridal gown, with the idea of being a bride, has a place in every tranny's closet and is certainly the most popular dress in ours. Still, I thought it a funny coincidence that these two messages arrived at practically the same moment. It crossed my mind that the two notes might have been sent by one person: that there was no actual gown, no eager student, but only an imaginative tranny who was attempting to involve me and the academy in an elaborate fantasy without paying tuition. Naughty, naughty. Or maybe the gown was for real and the seller had set up a variation of bait and switch, hoping to lure me into purchasing an odd-size dress by dangling the incentive of an eager bride just waiting at the altar. Before we had a chance to respond to either message, my deputy Miss Viqui, who books all our classes, received a call from a prospective student who not only wanted to be a bride but whose measurements also fit the gown that was offered. Michael was five foot six and 180 pounds. Yet another bride, and just the right size and height! This was almost too much, even for the academy, where it often feels like June is busting out all over. I had Miss Viqui set up an orientation appointment for Michael.

During our preliminary consultation Michael quivered in his business suit as he confided that to see himself as a bride was his ultimate fantasy. I suggested he open his shirt collar to make it easier to breathe, then I asked him if he had recently communicated with the academy via e-mail and he said no. It was clear he had not. I told him there was a very good chance I could find a gown to fit his femmeself, Diane, perfectly and instructed Michael to check back with us in five days. Michael left, giddy with excitement. Next, we telephoned Shelly, the seller. The voice at the other end of the phone was quite feminine. She was not a tranny and had worn the gown at her very own wedding.

Shelly arrived at the academy with a male friend. Shelly was tall and strong. A raven-haired amazon, she strutted in wearing a black leather jacket and blue jeans with a big set of keys dangling from her belt loop. She wore motorcycle boots. Shelly was a biker.

She removed the gown from the garment bag with the help of her companion, a young man in a beige three-piece suit a bit reminiscent of Tony Manero and *Saturday Night Fever*. His wavy brown hair just reached over his shirt collar. When he got a good look at the dress, he was taken aback. The gown was bright white, to the floor with lots of crinolines, lace, and tulip-shaped sleeves. The headpiece was a Juliet cap with a sheer white veil. "You wore that?" he asked.

"Yeah," replied our tomgirl sheepishly. "My grandmother made me. She took me to Kleinfeld's [the Brooklyn bridal mecca] to pick it out."

Shelly said that since her divorce a few years before, she had tried to sell the gown a number of times but without success. "How did you happen to connect with me?" I asked. One of her male biker friends, who knew of her desire to sell the gown, had been cruising the net and came upon our site. This did not surprise me at all, since I have spoken with quite a few Harley-Davidson types who sometimes swap their leathers for lingerie. Her friend told her about the academy and, voilà, now she was about to help make our student Diane/Michael's dream come true.

We negotiated a price, and then Shelly made a request. "My ex-husband told me that when he saw me in this dress coming down the aisle, he had an erection. I can think of no better comment on our marriage than to send him a photo of one of your students wearing the gown with his dick hanging out. I'll add a note and ask, 'Here, honey, does this still do it for you?'" I made no promise to Shelly about a photo. Her sentiment did not feel appropriately connubial. And I resolved that if Diane/Michael did consent to let me send a picture, I would make sure she looked real pretty.

A few days later we conducted the class with Diane. From the moment he walked through the door of the academy, Michael was in ecstasy. I welcomed him, and he wrapped his arms around me and hugged me the way a child hugs his mommy, pressing his cheek to one side to get that much closer to me. Michael was that grateful. It was all I could do to keep him from dropping to his knees. Actually, he did drop, but I made him get right up, as I don't encourage bowing and scraping.

As with many of the students, his exact age was difficult to guess. He looked much older at the start of class than he would look at its end. My first impression of him was "gray." Gray suit, gray hair, gray bra under his oxford shirt. We quickly got him out of all that and into a cheery pink dressing gown with ruffled white-lace trim. He had a little round tummy that we squeezed into a corset that redistributed the weight to give Michael as Diane some nice curves. As is our custom, we play music, and I gave Diane the choice from our assortment of female singers and composers. Sitting in the makeup chair, Miss Deborah doing his makeup, quiet, gray Michael began to shed not only pounds but years. He told us he loved Madonna. He'd taken his kids to her concert at the Meadowlands. He was rockin' and boppin'. " 'Like a virgin, kissed for the very first time. Like a vir-ir-ir-ir-gin—' " stopping to let Miss Deborah apply his lipstick. This was one happy campus queen. "Miss Vera, I feel like a virgin," he said.

"I hope so, Diane. You're not married yet."

Diane chose the longest wig in the academy collection. It was strawberry blond with the sides piled high on top. It would not have been my first choice—it was more Las Vegas showgirl than blushing bride—but when we saw her in it, the deans and I agreed that it was perfect. Diane/Michael's happiness was not subtle; there was no reason why her hairdo need be.

The wedding gown was, as I suspected, just the right size. Diane Michaels shivered as yards of taffeta, satin, and lace slid down her arms and over her torso. Her eyes filled with tears as she gazed at her reflection. It was a mirror moment. I wish I had a camera installed on the other side of the glass so that I could cap-ture Michael's first gaze and those of so many other students. Yes, academy work is fulfilling and creative. The money is definitely nice and the camaraderie with the deans is delightful. But it is those moments when the student looks into the mirror and her reflection lights up the room that are the icing on the cake, the gloss on the lipstick, the extra lift in the crinoline.

While Miss Tiger, ballet mistress, taught Diane how to walk down the aisle, the other deans and I pulled some academy frocks from the closet so our gowns would compliment Diane's in her wedding album. Diane had signed up for Miracle Miss, our four-hour class that involved dressing and photographing the bride, but Diane asked that we also have a small ceremony. It was important to her that we commemorate this day in a ritual and that someone be there to stand up for her, which I did. But I was just a surrogate. It was Michael who put on the dress, gave his femme-self, and married her too.

During the photo session, I asked Diane if she would enjoy posing for some more risqué boudoir shots that I could pass on to the original owner of the dress. She liked the idea and when I suggested she lie on a divan and reveal her penis under some ruffles and lace, she said the pose turned her on. Her tumescent penis served as punctuation. We took one Polaroid to send to Shelly and another for Diane. The only sad moment came at the end of the day when we had to take Michael out of the wedding gown. Oh, that he could be a bride every minute of the day. Oh, that we all could. Again I got that big hug. Michael suggested that I include a mention of the bridal option on the telephone greeting that first-time callers get when they contact the academy. It's been there ever since, and I am sure Michael calls often just to hear the words and relive his experience.

I sent the Polaroid of Diane Michaels en flagrante off to Shelly, who forwarded it to her ex-husband. I imagined him opening the envelope and seeing Diane Michaels in that wedding gown. I would not be surprised if he telephoned Shelly—which may be what she wanted her ex to do all along. In the course of the conversation he admits that he really would have loved to wear that gown himself. That instead of turning him off the picture of our student Diane in the gown turned him on. He imagined himself as the bride and his ex-wife walking beside him, not in a bridal gown but in trousers. She clearly liked wearing them a lot better. The picture would stimulate a new level of honesty between them and an eventual reconciliation. And one day wedding bells would chime again for that couple—only this time, the groom wears the dress. It still gives him an erection, and Shelly the biker goes for a ride.

Miss Vera with her academy supermodels (left to right): Joan, Patti, and Jennifer James (Photo by Jim Salzano)

CHAPTER 10

The School for Wives

his chapter is for all of the wives or significant others (SO's) whom I have met but have not had a chance to speak with as intimately as I would have liked. And for all of you whom I have not met because your partner is afraid to tell you how much he loves wearing a dress. This is for the wives who send me gifts and thank-you notes as well as for the wife who read my first book and said she wanted "to throw me across the room" and to other angry wives. This is also for a woman or man looking for a mate to let you know about a segment of the male population with a lot of sometimes shy but very eligible bachelorettes. I don't mean to overlook gay couples in this chapter, because I know there are gay men who are in the closet about cross-dressing. I had one gay partner call to thank me after his mate had come for a class and then revealed his femmeself to his lover. He said the honesty really deepened their relationship. So if you are in a gay relationship, I hope you will read this chapter and make your own translation.

Each year at the academy a small number of wives are involved in their husbands' classes. Some accompany their husbands to the school and participate either all or part of the time. Just recently Laurie encouraged her husband, Dee, to take a much needed vacation, a long romantic weekend in Manhattan. They spent three days in town, one of which was Dee's school day. While Dee was in class, Laurie went shopping, then we all went out for dinner at Lips, the tranny restaurant located in the West Village. Laurie was the most openly demonstrative wife we have had at the academy. She kissed Dee a number of times at the dinner table, and Dee just melted (emotionally, not cosmetically). Other wives who don't actually visit themselves chat with me beforehand just to be sure of who and what their husbands are getting involved in. Some hubbies would love to believe that their wives have demanded that they come to me for training and that, as obedient husbands, they have no choice but to comply (www.pinaforepages.com). That is their fantasy, but that has never been the case. A wife who participates is a generous and compassionate woman who understands that exploring this part of himself is important to her mate. From the wives whom I have encountered, I must also state that such a wife is usually self-confident, has a sense of adventure and certainly a sense of humor, trusts in her marriage, and knows she is loved. All this does not come easy. It helps if your mate has shared this not-insignificant detail about himself with you before you married, rather than surprised you ten years later with the news that your knight in shining armor wants to be your maid. Take heart: he can be both. There is some training involved, much more than teaching him what you would like for your breakfast in bed (though that's not to be sniffed at). Actually, it's really about compromise and communication, just like everything else that challenges your relationship. It is important to remember that you are not alone. There are a lot of resources available to you, as a couple and individually. This is not uncharted territory.

I won't presume to generalize. There are couples who are married for years before they confront the issue of cross-dressing. Some wives find out by accident; others have husbands who confide in them. At some point you will decide if this is a deal breaker or if the two of you want to stay married, and you may confront this decision more than once. Once your tranny is out of the closet, he is going to evolve and so will you. Not every marriage is meant to last. Some couples use the issue of cross-dressing as an escape from an already sinking ship. Other couples decide out of love and respect that it is better to proceed separately than together. And there are others for whom it can be a doorway to adventure and a tunnel deep into each other's hearts.

I would like to introduce you to Colleen H. I met Colleen and her husband, Phil, who is also known as Heather, when I was researching a story for *Marie Claire* magazine. About a year before I sat down to write this book an editor named Alison from the U.S. edition of *Marie Claire* telephoned me with an assignment. An article about our academy had been published in British *Marie Claire,* and now American *Marie Claire* wanted an article from the wife's point of view. They also wanted the couple to agree to be photographed, in other words to be "out." The article was for a particular slot, a first-person true-story tabloid kind of deal. Now to find the couples—not one but three, because Alison said the editor in chief, Glenda, wanted a choice. I rose to the challenge and through my contacts found three couples who were willing to share their lives. I sent in snapshots and backgrounds and waited a week. Nothing. One month later, still no decision. I commented to Alison that I thought this was really rude as these couples were being very generous with themselves to agree to this story in the first place and they deserved an answer as to who would be picked. Another month went by before Glenda made a choice. I interviewed Colleen H., who honestly revealed many of the pluses and minuses of being the wife of a cross-dresser. Alison said the story looked fine. Some time later, she sent about thirty questions, many of which were already answered to some degree in the text. Most of her questions were slanted to try to elicit negative answers. Colleen and Phil saw through all these questions, as I did. The magazine had its own agenda. Colleen said she was happy with the version of the story that I handed in and if *Marie Claire* wasn't, in essence they could shove it. I was paid for the story, but it never ran. All I could say afterward was, what a bunch of silly, uptight women and disappointing journalists. I am pleased to have the opportunity to present Colleen's story to you now.

My Husband, Heather

as told to me by Colleen H.

I thought nothing about my husband, Philip's, decision to do female drag for Halloween 1991. But something intrigued me about the careful way he put on his lipstick. Two months later as we lay in bed on New Year's Eve, he struggled to tell me something. He had been moody for weeks. Suddenly, that image of him looking in the mirror flashed in my mind. I burst out, "You want to be one of those cross-dressers, don't you?" He looked at me, his eyes big as saucers, amazed that I had guessed so correctly, and said, "Actually, I've been one my whole life."

I was totally shocked. My husband, Phil, and I are state office workers in Texas, but our passion is music. Phil is a macho roots rocker, guitar riding below the belt, groupies all around. Nothing in our love life led me to question he was anything but a red-blooded American male, nor does it today.

We had gotten together young, having met at work when he was twenty and I was seventeen and a senior in high school. We married right after my graduation from the University of Texas, where I majored in business and got a B.B.A. Philip had taken me to my senior prom. He saw me through college. He was the first person I ever had sex with, and I was the first for him. In 1991, he was twenty-seven and I was twenty-four. We had been together for seven years and married for two. We were not only husband and wife, we were best friends.

We talked all night. He told me that the earliest he remembered trying on women's clothes was when he was eleven or twelve. He snuck into his mother's closet and wore her party dresses, the frillier the better. When he was sixteen, she came home one day and discovered him in her wedding gown. She told him that she was ashamed of him and warned him that if he continued, she would tell his father. Philip's father traveled a lot in his job, so he was often away from home. His mother's angry threats did not stop Philip from dressing; he just became more cautious.

I was disappointed that Philip had not told me all this sooner. He was cross-dressing the whole time we were together and I didn't even know it. He hid it from me so completely. He explained that he was afraid I would leave him, plus he had hoped that once we got married, it would cure him. The feelings just got stronger. He knew that sooner or later he was going to have to tell me, but he didn't know how to go about getting information. Finally, he went to the library. In psychology books he read about transsexuals who want to change their bodies and transvestites, or cross-dressers, who just want to change their clothes. He identified himself as a heterosexual cross-dresser and found an address for a group called Tri-Ess (www.tri-ess.org) that, he learned, is the international support and social organization for heterosexual cross-dressers and their loved ones. He had written to Tri-Ess for materials and was prepared with plenty for me to read, including a newsletter called *The Sweetheart Connection* (www.rainbowtrail.info/), which was written by and for cross-dressers' wives and partners.

I was very lucky. Many women don't find out that way. I have heard all sorts of horror stories about women who find a woman's slinky garment—so they think their husbands are cheating on them—or they find some kinky magazine that isn't something they would want to read. A lot of husbands accidentally on purpose leave stuff around because they don't know how to tell their wives. I recommend men tell their fiancées before they are married. It is a trust thing.

The next morning at breakfast I was reading through the materials he had given me when he said, "I would like to show you what I look like with makeup on. Would you be comfortable with that?" I said, "Uh . . . okay." I didn't know what to expect. He was in the bathroom for about two hours, putting on makeup. When he finally came out, I was expecting clown makeup, but he didn't look half bad. I was shocked. I thought, "Gosh, he must have done this a few times." At first he was tense, but when he realized I wasn't going to throw him out of the house or order him to "take that crap off your face," he began to relax. That he had trusted me enough to tell me and that I had listened without judging him helped bring us even closer together. It never occurred to me to ask him to stop. I understood right away that this was a part of him and that I had better educate myself to the facts. I never thought that he was gay. I was too happy in our sexual relationship for that to be the case.

I asked him a lot of questions. How had he managed to dress without my knowing? Each Sunday, when I went off to do the grocery shopping, it was his job to vacuum and dust. He said that in reality, the house got a ten-minute vacuum and dust job and the rest of the time he was dressing. At the time, he was a lot heavier, and I could not imagine what he had found in my closet to fit him. I had to laugh when he told me he had stolen a half-finished dress that my mother had been sewing for me to wear as maid of honor for a friend who, instead, chose to elope. The dress didn't have the hem done or the zipper in, so it was longer and big enough. So he was wearing this god-awful purple taffeta thing. I said, "You're kidding me!

"Well, I guess you need something better to wear, don't you." He could not believe that I would suggest getting a dress for him. That was the first of what has turned out to be many shopping sprees. This first time Phil went as himself, or as we say, in drab. He wanted to go to a vintage store and find a floor-length, rustling ball gown with lots of crinolines, but I convinced him to go with something more up-to-date, so we visited a store called Weiner's. I guess the name was pretty ironic.

I must admit, as we shopped I was thinking, "This is all pretty weird. I can't believe I am doing this." We brought home this really pretty fall-colored long-sleeved knit dress, size large, that came down to the knee. The second thing he bought—which he purchased through one of those mail-order catalogs I have come to learn are so important in the life of a cross-dresser—was a corset. He wanted his body shape to be different. That too was weird.

The next thing I knew, I was ordering breast forms and a mastectomy bra from the JCPenney catalog (www .jcpenney.com). The salesperson was so very nice to me, it made me wonder. Then I realized that she probably thought I had breast cancer. Again, I thought, "This is really bizarre. Should I have told her as I ordered the breast forms, 'Don't worry, I don't have cancer. My husband just likes to wear a bra'?"

He put on the dress, the bra, and everything, and then I helped him with his makeup because he really wasn't good with that yet. He's real good with makeup now—in fact, he's better than I am. We curled his hair with teeny little rollers, and when I saw the whole picture I thought, "Wow, if I didn't hear his voice and I saw him across the room, I would think he looked pretty good."

Phil had been calling himself Phyllis when he was dressed. We continued to use Phyllis but eventually we changed his name to Heather. He is much more of a Heather, young and carefree. A month after Phil revealed his cross-dressing to me, we attended our first support group right in San Antonio. Now we usually go to two Tri-Ess meetings a month, one in Austin and one in Houston. I was pleased there was a wives' group there, as well, and

I thought, "This group is good for me, too." In the wives' group, feelings range from wives who are angry and can't stand their husbands cross-dressing to wives who are totally accepting. You can rave, rant, laugh, cry. The group isn't about changing anyone's mind, it is about support.

The first time Phil dressed as Heather and went out was for a CD meeting in another town. He did not really go out in public. It was more like my giving him a one-hour pep talk followed by Heather's mad dash from our hotel room to the car. He was so afraid.

One month later, which was just two months after Philip had revealed himself to me, we were attending our first cross-dressing convention. It was called the Texas T-Party, and I learned it was one of several cross-dressing conventions held throughout the year in major cities (www .ifge.org). We were surrounded by three hundred cross-dressers. Boy, was I thrown. A lot of these guys were like six foot five. There were fighter pilots, lawyers, firemen, construction workers, architects, doctors, musicians—oh, and lots of computer people—and they were all in very fancy dresses. It took place in San Antonio, away from home, so we decided to use the opportunity to really take Heather out. Phil said, "Okay, I am going to bite the bullet. We're going to do it." We went to a mall that the other conventioneers said was safe to visit. Cross-dressers are very security conscious. We weren't working at the time, so we had a lot more freedom than most people and I wasn't so concerned that we would run into anyone. He wore an outfit that he got at a tag sale. (When cross-dressers recycle their clothes they can get some great deals.) He had this outfit, a skirt and blouse, that looked really nice, but he was so nervous that he wore dark glasses inside the shady mall.

In the beginning going out wasn't fun at all because as much as my husband wanted to do it, he was afraid. If people are mean to me, I can let it roll off my back, but I wanted to shelter my husband.

After that first experience, it became progressively easier for us to go out in public. If my husband was read, he didn't die on the spot, he wasn't struck by lightning. And I realized that being read wasn't the end of the world either. After that, we started to have fun. Now we go all over: shopping, traveling in airplanes, dinner, department store dressing rooms, and finally, the ladies' rest room.

Fortunately for my husband, he's not tall. He's five foot eight and he wears flats or tiny heels when he is out. He doesn't wear stilts. And that all helps him to pass. He used to be heavier; now he's real slim. That, too, helps him to pass and is a health benefit.

When Phil first came out to me, he didn't wear a nightgown or anything like that to bed because he didn't want me to misconstrue or think that he wanted anything different from our sexual relationship. Now he does sometimes wear a nightgown. Sometimes I wear lingerie, most times not. I know he enjoys wearing something feminine to bed, and his dressing has created more of an equal sharing relationship in bed. It's not always him being the instigator. Sometimes it's me. There's more foreplay. Our sex is longer; it's more satisfying; he shares more intimately with me. We both get more out of it. And this change carries through even when we go to bed in our tee shirts.

I don't hold hands in public with Heather, though I do with Phil. One time, early on, I forgot myself. We were talking and joking with each other and I was touching

Heather's shoulder and hair, as lovers do. I wasn't thinking. Across the way, a woman was staring at us, giving us
the glare of a lifetime. She couldn't hear us, so I wondered how Phil got read. Then it dawned on me that she
thought we were two lesbians. At first, I thought it was
funny, but then I realized that I don't want to be misin-
terpreted. To be a lesbian is fine, but I am not a lesbian.
When we go out we are just two friends.

When he first came out, my husband wanted to be
Heather almost all the time. Gender euphoria. Whew! I
had a problem with that because I didn't want to dress up
all the time. I understood that he felt like he was being
let out of jail, but in order to be fashionably compatible
with Heather I had to wear lots of makeup, do my hair—
the whole nine yards—support panty hose, ugh. After
about the second month I said, "You've just got to get
this out of your system faster because I am tired. I don't
want to go to the mall in pumps five times a week." It
subsided.

Along the way there have been lots of things we
needed to work out, some big, some little. He didn't tell
me before he shaved his legs. Fortunately, I like the
change, but I made it clear that on most things I did not
want to be left out of the loop.

There was only one thing that really made me afraid.
In one group, the subject of hormones came up. A few
members were discussing dressing full-time and using
hormones. Some members who were on hormones even
raved about them. My husband, being newly out, was
very impressionable and started thinking that maybe he
should take hormones. I was scared, but I didn't let on. I
didn't blow up at him, I decided to use reason. When he

brought it up, I said, "You know you need to step back and really look at this. Is this really who you are? Is this really where you are with this? Do you want to do this? And if you continue to do this it will change your body. You will start growing breast tissue. Is that where this is headed?" I didn't say "I'm scared" or "You're crazy." I felt that, believe me, I felt that. He seriously thought about it and he said, "You know what, Colleen, you're absolutely right. This isn't me at all. I don't want to change my body."

I perform with my husband now. I didn't used to. I sing and I do percussion and I'm going to be doing keyboards. It's a rush. I think our being out about cross-dressing has helped me to do things like this. I think it has helped my self-esteem. I was the last of six children. I was a very sheltered person. I grew up in a very strict home. I never felt self-confident. I was always being compared to my brothers and sisters. I never felt good enough. Having shared this cross-dressing with my husband and knowing that he loves me and trusts me to really share this . . . and the stuff we've done. Within a few months after he told me, we were on a talk show. I never thought I'd get to do stuff like that. We've traveled. We've been in books. It's opened up possibilities for me that I never thought I'd be able to do. I've actually gotten more benefit out of it than anything. I've found that my role has been very positive. I've been able to help educate other wives or girlfriends who are just finding out.

When we are really close with friends outside the cross-dressing community, we tell them. I don't want to be leading a double life. I've not had contact with my family for various reasons for years, but his mom knows.

We told her together. We see her every week and each week she comes up with a different theory. She'll say, "Oh, it's because you were born a month premature." Or (and this is my favorite), "It's because you're a Gemini." Personally, I think my husband was just born this way.

His mother is seventy. She belongs to a different generation and there is a generation gap. I was born in the sixties—what can I say? We have friends in their thirties and their forties and their kids are growing up in a different atmosphere than they did. There are a lot more people coming out who are in their thirties and even in their twenties and that is hopeful to me. People sometimes bring their children to CD meetings. Our dedication to music has precluded us from raising a family. We don't want to do it on the road. We do have our little cat, Mouse, and she is totally out.

My husband is more sensitive to my needs when he is Heather. He has incorporated her so well into his personality that he really doesn't change when he puts on different clothes. Some people take a lot longer to find that balance. I believe it is important that I help him keep it, and our relationship has benefited. He has learned he can trust me with his needs and I make sure that he understands mine. I am glad that I take this active role in my husband's cross-dressing and that I can use that role to help educate people and break down stereotypes. We have thrived.

A year after I conducted this interview, Colleen and Phil/ Heather continue to progress. Colleen was proud of her promotion and pay raise. Phil was off to Germany for a few weeks for his first European gig. Heather is alive and well, as is Mouse the cat.

More Wives Speak

On the web page of tranny Jamie Faye Fenton (http:// members.tgforum.com/jamie/), who along with JoAnn Roberts and Cindy Martin helps run Transgender Forum (www.tgforum .com)—a site that needs to be on every tranny's list of favorites— you will find a link to a piece called "Even Genetic Girls Get the Blues" (http://members.tgforum.com/jamie/ggblues.html), which was written by Jamie's wife, E. Fenton. The piece offers sage advice mixed with some humor. E. Fenton says, "When I attended a meeting of SOs (significant others), I found that it helped immensely to speak to other women who were experiencing some of the same difficulties, fears, and frustrations. . . . It felt good to engage in the age-old sport of complaining about men, albeit with a different twist (e.g., "I hate it when he uses my makeup"). She lists and responds to some of the thornier issues:

- Am I not "feminine" enough?
- What about the time it takes away from us?
- I miss the presence of men, especially when he giggles on the phone with his "girlfriends."
- How to deal with cross-dressing overload.
- I'm scared. Where is this heading?
- What will my family or our neighbors think?
- I fear for his safety when he is out.
- Our sex life has suffered. I'm not a lesbian.

Among other solutions, Ms. Fenton's husband bought her a horse. "I have to hand it to him," she says. "He came up with an ingenious solution." It didn't solve all their problems, but it was on the right track.

In 1994, Frances Fairfax authored "A Wives Bill of Rights" in *The Sweetheart Connection,* the newsletter published by Tri-Ess Wives. It is a straightforward document with twelve points. One point reads, "We have the right to honest and open communication with our husbands, with negotiation and compromise on both sides, particularly in regard to allocation of family resources and in matters pertaining to telling our children. Old patterns of selfishness and deception must cease."

Another point reads, "We have the right to our husbands as men, the men we married, men who maintain a positive, healthy masculinity while 'exploring their feminity' and seek neither to evade responsibilities nor to appropriate our own feminine roles."

Her husband countered with twelve points from the cross-dresser's point of view.

Ms. Fairfax does not beat around the bush. This comes not from a martyr, suffering in silence. This comes from a woman determined to make her marriage work and to safeguard the happiness she signed up for when she said "I do." But in order to have a chance to express how you feel, your husband needs to clue you in to the real deal.

About 70 percent of the academy's students are currently married. Of those, about 10 percent are married for the second time. Most of those told their sweethearts about their cross-dressing before saying "I do," and those marriages are doing very well. However, many times when I ask a married student if he has shared his cross-dressing with his wife, he will say, "Oh, I can't. My wife would never understand." To me, what that means is the tranny doesn't understand, so how could he believe that his wife would be able to? My first goal is to help the student to understand so that he can feel more confident about revealing this fact to his partner.

Though your husband is a grown man, where his cross-dressing is concerned, he can still be a child. As a little boy he learned it was a very bad thing to put on girl's clothes. Oh, it might have been cute for a while, and it certainly served many protective purposes for him. And it always felt very, very good. But he learned to keep it a secret. Sometimes, the urge would pass. Many men lose interest in cross-dressing when they are courting, so they hope that when they get married this need will just go away. The way they see it, they did not withhold information from you when they wed. They honestly thought, and usually hoped and prayed, that their femmeself had gone off, maybe with some other guy. But, then, she's ba-a-ack. And you have a right to be pissed. From your point of view, as Colleen said, "It's a matter of trust."

How do you deal? You talk and you listen. You and your husband are both feeling fragile and vulnerable, so you can get only so much support from each other. Now is the time when talking to other CD wives is so helpful, just as it is important for him to connect with other trannies. Support groups are the best. Having been a member of Club 90, a five-member porn star support group, for sixteen years, I can attest to that.

Another, more private, way to get support is with the help of a counselor experienced in issues of sex and gender. Ads for their services can be found in Transgender Tapestry Magazine. Dr. Sandra Cole in Michigan has had lots of experience counseling couples on the subject of cross-dressing. She is now a part of Gender Education and Advocacy (www.gender.org). Dr. Kit Racklin in New York is also very experienced, as are New York psychotherapists Barbara Warren and John Capozuca.

What About Sex?

One of the questions to ask right off the bat is if there is any change to be expected in your sex life. Keep in mind that your husband may not really know the answer to this question, though he may give one anyway. So you've got to stay alert to your own needs and communicate them. This can be a very wonderful sexually experimental time for you and your husband. Recently, I heard from Bette. Her husband had told her about his cross-dressing six months before we spoke. She called me, asking for makeup tips and from there we got down to other topics of interest. "So how is your sex life?" I asked.

Bette told me that ever since her husband confided in her, they'd been "doing it almost every night." She said before that their sex life had dwindled to almost nothing. "I was ready to throw in the towel." Then from the famine to the feast. But, for Bette, every night was too much of a good thing. We agreed that she could tell her husband so and see what response that elicited. Maybe now that he had spoken up, he felt he had to prove his love every night. Or maybe now that this part of his sexuality was revealed, the floodgates had opened and he was more sexually liberated and joyful. Some pillow talk would help. For one thing, their marriage was alive again. I heard it in Bette's voice. She was very excited to be going to their first support group meeting. Her husband had asked if he could go dressed, and she thought that was a great idea and was helping him with his makeup. And that's how she happened to call me.

Mommy Dearest

When I say, "Be alert to your needs," I have a few specifics in mind. Any wife, whether she is married to a cross-dresser or not, wrankles when she is being put in the position of being her husband's mother. You are not his mom; you are not a dominatrix to order him around (unless you want to be); and you are real, not a fantasy. Just as he has a right to have sex in a nightie, you have a right to be naked if you choose and neither one need apologize. I once had a student tell me his wife was his "queen." I told him that sounded very nice but just remember she is a flesh-and-blood woman. She is not perfect, her seams are not always going to be straight, and she has real human needs, one of them being a compatible sex partner.

I do not think that sex is a cure for everything. But I do believe that if a couple has a compatible sex life, they have a good chance of staying together. I choose the word "compatible" because I know that we all have different sexual needs and desires. My question is, Are you each getting your needs and desires met? We'll continue that discussion in sex ed. class.

How to Connect

So what networks are out there for wives and significant others? Tri-Ess International is set up as a huge sorority for heterosexual cross-dressers and their loved ones with chapters in cities across the country and abroad. The chapters run meetings that include meetings for significant others, as Colleen has already mentioned. Tri-Ess publishes a monthly magazine, *The Mirror,* and wives and partners can get together online at the CDSO Forum (www.rainbowtrail/info). The Renaissance Transgender Association (www.ren.org) also has local chapters in some states and is not as strictly heterosexual in its orientation as Tri-Ess. There are several dozen transgender conventions held in major cities throughout the year. The tranny calendar is quite full. SPICE is an annual conference held each summer run by and for cross-dressers' wives (www.tri-ess.org/spice). Men are welcome at SPICE but only in male attire. Tri-Ess conventions often include meetings for Tri-Ess Kids, who have recently come up with their own bill of rights.

All this sounds pretty straight. What if you want to explore? It can happen that as your husband begins to experience his female liberation, you can feel more open to experimentation. Many hip and wonderful parties take place annually: New York's Black and Blue Ball, Ms. Antoinette's Dressed to Thrill Ball in Las Vegas, San Francisco's Exotic Erotic Ball (www.exoticeroticball.com), and the Los Angeles Fetish Ball. You may bring out the inner butch or inner bitch and free a new sexpot within.

Some couples choose to open their marriage to polyamory, the practice of being in a committed and loving relationship with more than one person. Loving More (www.lovemore.com) is a national organization dedicated to that purpose. It is not a swing club; in fact, not all of these relationships are sexual. The group includes trios, extended families, open marriages, and committed singles—all of whom share love and intimacy with more than one person.

You have a lot of options to explore.

Dr. Annie Sprinkle and Miss Vera
(Photo from the author's collection)

CHAPTER 11

Sex Education

et's begin sex education class with the removal of the word "should." No matter what genes, chromosomes, hormones, or genitalia you were born with or without, there are no rules as to what your sexual orientation will or "should" be. Sexual orientation is who you feel attracted to, who you choose as a sex partner. You can choose anyone, and sometimes you surprise even yourself. You can also be celibate. Though, from what I have seen, many people living in the state of celibacy would prefer to relocate. Life might be so simple if you were attracted to only your physical opposite. We could concentrate on perpetuating the species and get on with it. But nature is messy, at least to our understanding, and to paraphrase Camille Paglia in *Sexual Personae,* sex is nature inside of us. From what I have come to know in my research and from my own private laboratory here at the academy, you, my dear tranny—and all of us—have the potential to be a lot of different people sexually. To try to confine yourself to one little box can be like setting the table for two and having six guests arrive for dinner. Somebody is bound to end up hungry. Remember that quote from *Auntie Mame,* the one that Miss Viqui cited in her bio: "Life is a banquet and most poor bastards are starving to death." Often, the one left starving is your femmeself. You would not treat her like Little Orphan Annie and keep her wearing the same old dress, so don't leave her begging for scraps from the sexual smorgasbord.

Part of the reason your femmeself exists is to free you from the confines of your male persona. To expect her to obey the same rules of sexual behavior as him is to shortchange yourself. You may have tried to eliminate her and may even have shooed her away for a time. Until one day, she's back, yowling for attention like a hungry pussy cat. She is your inner slut, your inner goddess, your inner madonna and whore, your erotic mother—and her goal is to bring you home to who you are. She visits you on the path of your imagination. When you wrap her in a nightie or a slip . . . panties . . . heels . . . you acknowledge her existence, you begin to make her real. How far you go when you turn the woman of your dreams into a material girl is up to you, the whole you.

Student Brett, in a short story, "First Time Out," wrote: "He had decided. Tonight was the night. . . . Now after twenty years Travis was going to allow Rebecca out into the world to see what she would do. He was going to let her take over, just for one night." And then later, "She was going to tease him and make him squirm throughout the transformation. She wanted to take over for good. . . ." In this fantasy, Rebecca leads Travis to places and experiences he would not have known without her, but she never gets there without him.

Girl Guides

Letting your femmeself be a guide will help you to learn to trust yourself. Of course, you will need to exercise common-sense rules: practice safe sex and don't take unfair advantage of another person or engage in nonconsensual sex. I am not suggesting you be reckless or hurtful, but I am saying do experiment and explore. Whether you are living a straight lifestyle, gay lifestyle, bi, tranny, or a combo, other people will be only too eager to tell you who you are. They have their own agendas, and will want to categorize you according to what suits their fancy or fantasy. It's fine to accept ideas into your sexual suggestion box, but you are in charge of the final tally.

By eliminating "should" from your sexual vocabulary, you can concentrate on pleasure. You can evolve and grow. No matter what gender role you are in—male, female, or transgender—you can have sex with a partner from any other gender. People do. Whether you choose to or not is a different matter. You may have other considerations, depending on other choices you have made in your life. If you are in a committed relationship, you may choose to be monogamous but let your fantasies run wild.

Miss Barbara, our dean of femmenergy, encourages you to think of yourself as a source of energy without a label. Miss Kate, our dean of hearts and gender outlaw, encourages you to be your own shero or a supertranny, ready to cut through shackles to free your heart. Miss Eva, our dean of seductive arts, encourages you to learn every flirtatious trick in the book, to use your body as a subtle tool to express your eroticism.

Just how important are your clothes to your sexuality? Plenty. Perhaps you are one of those trannies who says, "Cross-dressing, for me, is not about sex—it's about gender" or "It's about glamour." Cross-dressing helps you to better express who you are, your true nature, and there is a sexual element in that. Or you may say, "Cross-dressing is all about sex for me. Just give me a pair of panties and I'm in heaven. I don't need another person." That is certainly an option. But I suggest that you let the pleasure you experience from your slinky clothes be a dynamic experience, not an end in itself. Let the pleasure flow in and out of you. Miss Eva teaches you how to work those props and work that body. Hold someone's attention with your eyes, just for a moment. Touch your hand to the softness of your blouse, just near your throat, oh so close to a button. Slide your hands down your skirt along your hips as you sit. Your clothes have proven themselves to be an important part of your sexuality, a trigger, and you have a right to bear arms.

When I teach sex ed., I like to get down to basic questions and answers: What has been your sexual experience? Do you have a significant other—female, male, or tranny? Do you share your femmeself with your partner? Would you like to? What are your fantasies? How do you feel about your body? Shall we design a vulva for you from this book of photographs called *Femalia*? Or are you afraid it might bite? Shall we go to the sex-toy shop and get some school supplies? Watch an illustrative video, read a book, find the right vibrator or dildo for you to use at home? How about a trip to the masseuse or masseur? Ours is the practical school of sex education, taught by teachers who practice what we preach.

Tantric sex, the province of Miss Barbara, is based on the idea of sexual energy, or kundalini, traveling on your breath, filling not only your body but also your spirit. Kundalini is considered a female energy, so it is very appropriate that kundalini enters your body in the finery of your femmeself. Sex is not only the way we procreate, it is also the way we play. For centuries, work has been considered the province of men and play the province of women.

And women have become the great sex teachers of today. Let your femmeself be one, too. Let her teach you to play—play doctor, if you will. Like one of the great sex teachers, newly appointed (congratulations!) Annie Sprinkle, Ph.D., has said, sex heals. Are you ready for some sexual healing, little sister?

Times have changed since the days when sex information was dispensed only in an antiseptic clinic or an adult bookstore on the run-down side of town. Today's most influential erotic entrepreneurs are women. Good Vibrations (www.goodvibes.com) in San Francisco was created by Joani Blank and is now owned by its female employees. Good Vibes gave birth to the Sexuality Library that offers books and produces videos, such as the best-selling *Bend Over, Boyfriend* and *Bend Over, Boyfriend 2,* in which Dr. Carol Queen and her partner, Robert Morgan, demonstrate the joys of anal sex. Such videos and DVDs are great ways for you to share your until-now secret fantasies with a partner.

Here is an example of how we used one in class.

Bombs Away

Where were you when you learned we bombed Baghdad? I know these days, unfortunately, it is difficult to keep track of whom we are bombing. But that day I remember vividly. At the academy we were engaged in sex education class with student Christina Rosalita Starr and his wife, Jill, both in their early thirties. Christina as Ross is a vice president of a very large Midwest corporation; Jill is a lab researcher. This was Christina's second visit to the academy for a two-day femme intensive. The previous year, Ross had arrived with Jill's blessing and a small but tasteful wardrobe that she had helped him choose. The deans and I especially loved Christina's black sweater with faux-leopard collar and buttons. For his second course, Jill had decided to accompany Ross to Christina's world. Christina's wardrobe was more extensive, and she now owned a vibrating dildo the color of cotton candy that Jill knew about but had never seen. On the first day of lessons, we transformed Ross into Christina. The deans supervised Christina Rosalita's classes and took her out shopping. We also did a makeover on Jill, giving her a new, more sophisticated hairdo. Then we went out for a night on the town.

Sex education class was scheduled for day two, and Jill had decided that she wanted to be included. She told me that she was not sure how far she would go in Christina's sex education class, that she would probably prefer to observe. I decided to test the waters with a video—that way we could all be voyeurs. I chose *Bend Over, Boyfriend* in which Dr. Queen, her mate, Robert, and a host of dildo-dipping lovelies treat their boyfriends to the joys of anal penetration while extolling its health benefits and explaining the safest and most pleasurable procedures. Miss Barbara joined us for the screening. As we began, our student Christina sat on her chair and lovingly caressed her pink toy.

We watched as Dr. Carol explained the positive aspects of penetration and Robert gazed adoringly up at her and enthusiastically agreed.

"Do *you* want that up inside you?" Jill asked her cross-dressed mate. "I thought you wanted it in your mouth?" Christina kept mum. Jill turned to me and said, "My husband has told me that his ultimate fantasy is to perform oral sex on himself as Christina."

"Oh, yes!" Christina enthused, clearly glad to have the subject shift to fellatio. "I know it must sound very self-centered, but I have often had the dream that my femmeself makes love to my male self, in particular, oral sex."

Though that may not surprise you, dear student, because I

have learned this is a somewhat popular fantasy with academy girls.

"Just look at this toy," said Christina. "Doesn't it look like a lollipop? Doesn't it make you want to eat it?" Christina was tactfully trying to diffuse the situation. We all knew we were not talking about sucking lollipops. And it wasn't much of a stretch to imagine Christina might fantasize about being down on her knees in front of a gentleman or a lady other than himself.

I suggested to Christina that she give us a demonstration. So while Jill, Miss Barbara, and I watched, Christina gave the dildo a good licking. I complimented her oral technique, as did Jill who said that she has received much pleasure from Christina's tongue. Okay, we had found mutual ground. Jill was being very supportive and Christina very considerate.

Now the video had shifted from talking to a scene where there was considerably more action. A young couple was having anal sex. She wore a harness and dildo. He was bent over, facing the camera, the pleasure of each slow thrust reflected on his face.

Jill and Christina Rosalita watched the video intently, while each stole glances at the other. Christina, emboldened by the movie, said she would like to experience penetration. Jill said she was not quite ready to participate herself, but that it was fine with her if Christina wanted to pleasure herself in that way. It was very important to Ross that his wife be aware of his activities. He did not want to feel that he was doing something on the sly. I don't think it is necessary to reveal every fantasy or masturbation technique to your partner, not by any means. But if you are hoping to eventually share something a bit more exotic with your lover, it can be a good idea to introduce the idea gradually. Miss Christina Rosalita was definitely hoping to one day share her toys with Jill.

We watched the video as a young man learned to slide first his finger inside his anus and then replace his finger with a firm, well-lubricated dildo. I thought a hands-on demonstration might be too intense for our couple at this point, so Christina was instructed to perform the same exercise as a homework assignment. "Take some private time and turn it into a meditation," I said, "then give me a report." Which she promised to do. Just then the telephone rang. It was Miss Kate, who informed me that we were now at war with Iraq and bombing Baghdad. I decided to keep the news to myself until after class. I thought that Christina and Jill had enough to think about. At the academy, we value Venus envy over penis envy. Make love, not war. If we have anything straight, it's our priorities. For Christina Rosalita and Jill, we—Miss Barbara, the video *Bend Over, Boyfriend,* and I—were catalysts to help bring them together.

Boston Tea Party

Another great erotic entrepreneur who offers a safe yet exciting place for couples and individuals is Kim Airs. Kim is the proprietress of the Grand Opening Sexuality Boutique in Brookline, Massachusetts (www.grandopening.com). Each month Kim hosts any number of workshops. Her lineup includes courses with names that are often self-explanatory, like "Bi Bi Love, Bi Bi Happiness"; "If, ands, and Butts"; "Creative Bondage"; "Erotic Writing"; "How to Talk to Your Kids About Sex"; "Stripping for Women" (her most popular offering); "Drag for Women," and many more, taught by invited experts. Some, like "Drag for Women," Kim teaches herself. She's got a male alter ego named Leo, who appears to be a refugee from those old-time porno dens and adult bookstores. Kim's place is quite the opposite of those drab spots. It's lovely and bright.

On the day I was invited there to teach, we had a Boston tea party. Kim had invited me to make a weekend of it: to ride with her in Boston's Pride parade on Saturday and to host Miss Vera's Tea Party for Boys Who Want to Be Girls the next day. I invited Patti Harrington to accompany me. I thought she deserved to ride down the street in the middle of the Pride march in a convertible. Unfortunately, Mother Nature had other plans. By ten A.M. on Saturday morning Boston's streets were flooded. For the first time in Boston Pride history, the parade was canceled. But no one was going to rain on our parade. The tea party must go on.

Kim's friend Miss Syd, a girl/girl, played hostess in a real Lucy Ricardo fifties flared dress and apron. She had decorated the shop for the occasion. It was pouring outside, but inside was a floral garden, thanks to Syd. I wasn't sure how many souls would brave the elements to spend some time with us. The rain finally let up, and some students began to arrive. It was a tight little band, and an interesting microcosm.

Stephanie was right on time. She had heard about our visit via the Tiffany Club (www.tcne.org), a transgender social group in nearby Waltham. Stephanie wore a white cotton dress covered with tiny flowers and white summer sandals, the perfect tea party ensemble, and a very bold outfit for the day. She sipped tea and made polite conversation, our Miss Prim. I complimented her on her ensemble. And she asked if I could suggest any improvements. She was almost perfect, except that her breasts were a bit too close to her chin. We decided to demonstrate the correction a bit later in class.

Karen was not so fashionable—her wrap skirt and knitted tee were not too exciting but actually more appropriate to the weather. Her wig was too short to frame her face properly. But she'd done a pretty good job with her makeup, and she possessed an air of tranquillity that bespoke more experience with her femmeself than implied by her fashion statement. Both Karen and Stephanie were married.

Vicky straddled the fence in girl's jeans and a top. His unadorned male face was framed by long, flowing tresses. Vicky boasted he could endure long hours confined by a corset and was thrilled when I chose him to be the corset model and laced him in nice and tight. Vicky was Miss Kink.

Eric was in total male clothes, or as we say, "drab." He loved to wear lingerie but made a strong point of saying he was a heterosexual looking for love. Anytime a reference to bi or homosexuality was made, Eric's face twisted in pain. I surmised he felt a strong urge to come to class but was afraid of what might be behind that urge. He was in his twenties, and this was his first baby step toward opening that closet door.

Then there was Bill. Okay, Bill was a trip. He had a big paunch, sandy hair, and an exuberant grin. Bill looked like he would be more at home with a brew and the ball game. He wore jeans and a tee shirt, and all that was missing was a Red Sox cap. Did he want to cross-dress? Did he want to be a cross-dresser's boyfriend? I could not be sure and neither could Bill. By the time class was dismissed he had been measured for his very own corset and had told Patti he would love to show her the town. Go figure.

There were also three couples. Barbara and Steve arrived for the introductory first hour, the tea party chat. When I asked how they happened to come that afternoon, Steve said he had been invited by Barbara, who was on Kim's mailing list. Steve looked terrified, and after a very short stay he and Barbara hightailed it out of there—hopefully, to go home and play dress-up.

Maxine and Kathy were delighted to participate. They had been looking forward to the class for months. In fact, they had introduced themselves to me in Las Vegas, where we all had attended Ms. Antoinette's Dressed to Thrill party. Maxine—born Mike and a former Marine with the tattoos to prove it—was a voluptuous sexpot. There was role reversal going on in the makeup department. Kathy wore very little, and Maxine wore enough for two. The couple had an active and adventuresome sex life and ran their own workshops where they encouraged other couples who showed an interest to explore forms of body modification, like piercing, and bondage and discipline with them.

Toby and Rob opened a new window on coupledom. She was small and boyish, he was tall and femme. They were together and they were a gender fuck. They were a couple of the here and now and the future.

For two hours we got to know one another. Kim gave her advice on choosing dildos for anal play. "Be sure to pick one with a wide flange, so you don't lose it inside you." Eric asked how to tell a woman he liked that he was into lingerie. "Tell her before you get married," said Karen and Stephanie. "Inform yourself about cross-dressing, so you can speak with an air of confidence and keep the discussion light," I offered.

Patti was an incredible assistant. I asked her if she would mind lifting her skirt to reveal some of her bodybuilding secrets. "Would you like me to take off my dress?" she asked, lowering her very practical long back zipper and slipping out of her lovely chiffon. Vanna White could not have done it better.

Taking it all down was Sarah, a reporter for the *Boston Phoenix* newspaper. She was getting quite a story. Her presence meant that with the power of the press we would reach many more people. I hoped she was up to her task because the students were so generous with themselves. The group represented so many different kinds of people, all with at least some common threads—not only the desire for nylons and silks but also the desire to revolt against gender barriers and encourage the evolution of new possibilities for life, liberty, and the pursuit of happiness. Just like at that other Boston tea party.

A Coach for Cinderfella

You may need some coaching in order to reveal your sexual desires, even to yourself. There are a number of options, depending on how physically involved you want to get with your coach. You can talk with a sex therapist or counselor like Dr. Patti Britton (www.yoursexcoach.com) or find a counselor through the American Association of Sex Educators, Counselors and Therapists (www.aasect.org). Sex therapy has come a long way since Dr. Freud. It's no longer the stepchild of psychiatry or psychology; it is a recognized field with very knowledgeable practitioners, many of whom did lots of research and personal exploration during the sixties sexual revolution before they ever cracked a book on the subject. Dr. Marty Klein (www.sexed.org) has been a licensed marriage and family counselor and sex therapist for over twenty years. He works with individuals and couples and lectures around the country, and offers a stimulating and well-thought-out newsletter called *Sexual Intelligence,* if you would like to keep abreast of the latest developments. You can be very frank when looking for a therapist and there is no need to settle for anyone with whom you feel uncomfortable. You can shop for a counselor as carefully as you shop for the right prom dress.

What if you would like a more hands-on form of treatment? Professional sex workers can be a great help. We will grow and grow up as a society when we recognize the benefits provided by hookers, thus acknowledging the tremendous variety of our sexual needs and desires. Here are some of the ways I see you students benefiting from the services of members of the world's oldest profession.

1. Adult virgins who need to have access to sex professionals who can help them experience sex for the first time.
2. Adults who feel ready to try a change in their sexual orientation, i.e., the male cross-dresser who until now has had sex only or mostly with women but feels a strong need to have sex with a man or another transgendered person.
3. Couples who would like to enhance their sex lives by inviting a third person, i.e., a sex professional, into their relationship.
4. Couples who choose to have "separate vacations" during which one or both partners uses the services of a sex professional.

It may take a bit of research through friends or the pages of sex papers such as San Francisco's *Spectator, Screw* magazine in New York, or the alternative papers and magazines that list escort services, but you are likely to find a treasure. There are also some very brilliant and compassionate dominatrixes who love to work with couples. Miranda and his significant other, Jane, visited the academy shortly before a visit to the West Coast. They wrote me a thank-you note and told me that while in San Francisco they enjoyed the time they spent with a dominatrix. Look for one who seems to love what she does and who won't run a guilt trip on you. Guilt can be an aphrodisiac. But if you continue to wrap your sexuality in guilt or shame—those feelings that began in your childhood—it will be difficult for you to evolve and offer yourself to another person as a giving, mature, and exciting lover. Guilt can also be very boring.

Your Sex Appeal

Trannies are sexy. I want you to take that in, believe it.

Eddie Izzard announces that he's a transvestite and he has a multitude of hip young women falling at his platform pumps. You don't have to be a slim, exotic "girlie boy" to be attractive—though I don't want to overlook that beautiful population. I interviewed a lot of "pre-ops" when they worked in the peep shows of Times Square.

As Miss Eva, our dean of seductive arts, says, "Every woman has a unique beauty. When you find that beauty, your power is limitless." At clubs like New York's Trannie Chasers and Edelweiss, girls with something extra are lusted after. Some cross-dressers want to be with other cross-dressers. And, yes, women are attracted to trannies, too. There is a network of women attracted to men who cross-dress. One of their organizers introduced herself to me at a benefit screening of *The Tranny School,* the documentary about our academy. I was so pleased to learn about these young women who appreciate a girl with something extra. Unfortunately, I do not have their URL but I am issuing an invitation to them now to get in touch with me.

Here is a letter I received from a young woman in her twenties.

Hi, Miss Vera,

I just had to skip class today to watch the show on the Metro Channel *The Tranny School.* Ever since Wigstock '94 (I was thirteen) I've thought, what a wonderful thing that men can express themselves in such a feminine way. Not even just feminine, just natural. . . . I'm a girl who wants guys to let loose and stop wearing the pants for once!

Sincerely,

C——

I have said that we all have the physical capacity to enjoy bisexual pleasure. Whether you choose to or not is a matter of the heart and mind. To find out more, you can visit Bi the Way (www.bitheway.org).

Some fantasies are meant to be realized, others not. One thing fantasies are not meant to be: policed. When you fill out an academy enrollment application, I ask you to tell me a short version of your favorite sexual fantasy. Here is one that arrived recently that I and Miss Eva, who was assisting me that day, found inspiring.

My favorite sexual fantasy is to be made love to as a woman by a woman. I meet a beautiful woman in a bar. We talk, getting friendlier and finally flirting a bit. She tells me that she is really excited by men who dress in lingerie and that she keeps lingerie for her lovers in her closet. I feel that I could faint at this news and soon follow her out of the bar and to her car. There we kiss and touch for the first time. At her place, she takes control, pushing me slowly, slowly into her bedroom, where she proceeds to pull out panties, a bra-slip, panty hose, pumps, and a wig. She helps me to undress and then slowly helps me get dressed in her lovely lingerie. All the while we kiss and touch. When I'm dressed, she invites me to her bed, where I begin to kiss her everywhere. I pull her panties aside and make love to her with my mouth. I feel that I could do this for hours. After her orgasm (or perhaps two or three) she tells me that she wants to return the favor. She exchanges my panty hose for a garter belt and stockings, freeing my clit; she kisses me softly, and tells me to wait while she slips into something. She disappears for a few minutes, returning in a body stocking and lovely strap-on dildo. I can't believe how turned on I am by this and immediately move to suck her beautiful cock. She finally stops me, lovingly pushing me back on the bed and spreading my legs. She rubs her cock on my clit and finally, spreading my legs even further, enters and makes love to me.

Meet the Bachelorettes

The deans and I are the subject of many a schoolgirl's crush, and we want to share the wealth. All of the following girls are easy to assemble and come with operating instructions. It's all part of my job!

Bachelorette 1, Jonelle, 40, unmarried. A bit shy but eager to please a woman; 5'10", very nice physique; keeps himself in shape touring on his mountain bike; excellent chef, Italian a specialty; well-paid, responsible job in communications industry; sexy bald pate; open to new experiences; a peach ripe for picking; enjoys wearing panty hose and has quite an impressive third leg.

Bachelorette 2, Priscilla, 47, divorced. Devoted dad; 6'0", living on his own in a lovely home with a huge library; historian; never at a loss for words but could be silenced by a pair of thighs wrapped round his smiling face; a daredevil and deep-sea diver; loves traveling to unusual places, most recently the Galápagos; owns his own company; loves to give and receive presents; enjoys wearing a pretty dress at home and while driving; a real romantic; would love a strong, confident woman to sweep him off his feet.

Bachelorette 3, Roberta, 18, yes that's right! New girl in town; student; very handsome; 5'9", dark hair and eyes; very embarrassed about his desire to dress; needs to have some fun and experience the wild side of life; well-brought-up gentleman who opens the door; too young to be sexually boxed in. Won't you please help lead this good girl astray?

Bachelorette 4, Lita, 33. 6'2", good-looking; hip music producer; lives with supportive, adventuresome girlfriend who opened his closet door; he's bisexual and feels energetic in female panties underneath his trousers; loves to entertain at home as well as travel to sunny climes; looking for Mr. Right to make it a threesome.

If you are a bachelorette looking for a mate, or a person who would like to meet a girl with something extra, I invite you to send a short description of yourself, along the lines of the above to crossdress@missvera.com.

Little Patrick, always a straight shooter (Photo courtesy of Patricia Harrington)

Patricia Harrington (Photo by Victor Carnuccio)

CHAPTER 12

The Patti Project

*T*rannies have a lot to teach the world. I've learned a lot from my students. One of the students who has taught me plenty is Patricia Jane Harrington. Patricia has referred to me as her other mother, though "godmom" or "midwife" is probably the better term. She's the daughter I never had. (Had I physically given birth to her, it would have been at an impossibly young age.) Instead, she emerged full grown. Today, her cheeks are smooth after two years of electrolysis, her eyebrows narrowed and neatly shaped. A mane of long natural hair cascades across her shoulders. Her hormone-induced breasts are just large enough for an A cup and big enough to make a curve in her sweater. She is a transgendered woman 24/7, and she is one of my best girlfriends.

Patricia is quite different from the Patrick who enrolled at the academy in 1993. Patrick was thirty-eight years old and a virgin, a fact I thought remarkable at the time, but less so now that we have had other unopened blossoms arrive at our door. He did highly specialized computer programming for a large metropolitan hospital and was very good at his job. Pat was a Deadhead and had a collection of concert ticket stubs to prove it. His wardrobe consisted of Grateful Dead tee shirts and jeans. At the end of a normal workweek, he'd join his buddies at a rowdy Irish bar where they listened to Gaelic rockers like Black 47. Pat was six foot four, painfully shy and joyless.

Then Pat put on a dress. It wasn't the first time. Like many trannies—maybe you—as a young boy he'd raided his sister's drawers. More recently he had visited an S/M parlor where he was feminized in a slapdash sort of way, but the experience wasn't to his liking. His visit to the academy was very significant. Afterward, he confided that when he went home that night, he stared for hours at the Polaroids of himself en femme. Pat began to visit the academy faithfully each month. He became very adept at his makeup. His posture improved. He excelled in all of his classes but one—sex education.

Our sex education department has greatly expanded since those early days. We now offer a multilevel curriculum: Miss Eva teaches the subtle and empowering art of flirting, Miss Barbara Carrellas is an expert in tantric yoga, and gender outlaw Kate Bornstein has had genital reassignment surgery and teaches from that perspective. But at the time of Pat's matriculation, the sex ed. department was in its most rudimentary stage, a simple hands-on experience. I felt it important that a student be comfortable accepting cross-dressing as part of his sexuality, so the class consisted of my talking the tranny through an orgasm while the student caressed her big clitoris or "girlcock." Not all opted for this part of their training, especially on a first visit. Others, as you might imagine, were quite enthusiastic and welcomed me as a sort of erotic cheerleader. Pat balked.

When I brought up the possibility of the sex ed. class for Patricia, she found reasons to avoid it. Finally, I convinced her to try. She could not come for quite a while, until she rolled over on her belly. I thought it was because she was more comfortable not looking directly at me as I observed. After class, Pat told me it was because he preferred not to look at his penis. "I hate that thing," he said. I felt so sad that Pat could feel that way about a part of himself. But what I did not understand was that for Patricia her penis was a foreign object. That first sex ed. class proved to be traumatic for Pat, and it was two years before he would consider another one. I was still determined to deflower this virgin, but I knew it would have to be through another route.

In the meantime, Pat's lessons in other areas continued. He had chosen the name Patricia, but to me the name sounded a bit too sophisticated and, well, *patrician*. "Patti" seemed to fit better because it was a happier name and Pat was becoming a happier person. The name "Patti" was also gender neutral and Patti seemed to be in this middle state, no longer Pat—the name associated with his male life—and not quite Patricia—our sort of spirit of Christmas to come. Patti was a model student, literally. In 1994, along with student Jennifer James, Patti was one of the academy's spokesmodels, appearing in our award-winning ad campaign and other media, such as an academy profile on HBO's *Real Sex*.

Patti admits, "I really had to learn more about myself before I could deal with my sexuality." I know it was also very important that Patti and I established a deeper level of trust. Two years later, I brought up the subject of sex fantasies over dinner. Patti told me that she dreamed of being tied up by a man who would splay her across a bed and have his way with her. Since she mentioned a male partner, I decided to find Mr. Right. That was the name of the dildo that was the right size to fulfill her. Pat told me he had tried to penetrate himself once before, but had stopped because it was too painful. In sex ed. class, I instructed Patti in how to avoid pain and experience pleasure. This time, she was a much more enthusiastic student.

Miss Vera's Pointers for Pleasurable Penetration

1. Lubrication of dildo.
2. Lubrication of anus.
3. Push out at the same time dildo is being inserted.

Patti adds:

1. "Relax and just go with it. It's a lot easier when you don't try to force things."
2. "You can give a lot of pleasure to your partner by contracting your sphincter around him. And, in turn, you will have more pleasure."

After seeing Pat's response to Mr. Right and learning of his fantasies, I thought it important for him to actually be touched by a man, but now I was careful not to make any assumptions. I wanted to ease him into it. I arranged for Patti to have a class with Samuel Kirchner who founded In Touch Therapy. Samuel has his male and female energies well balanced. He is a very wise and sensitive teacher who combines talking with the simplest physical activities like his workshop entitled "Walk into the Present." In Patti's case, all Samuel did was run his finger across her palm. This small action left her tingling from head to toe. The next thing

I knew Pat told me he had forsaken the Irish bars and was heading down to Uncle Charlie's—at the time, the most popular gay bar in the Village. Pat had grown up with a lot of internalized homophobia; letting a man touch you was actively discouraged. Once he had that experience, he wanted more. Now I had to step lively to keep up with him.

If our virgin was going to be cruising gay bars, I needed to make sure he knew all about safe sex. So I took Patti to a more traditional body worker, Hank the masseur.

In Hank's cozy studio, I hung back and observed. Hank gave Patti the option: "Shall I do the massage naked or dressed?" "Whichever you prefer," said the eager student. She was ready for anything. Hank's member stood out like a hat rack. His erection inspired Patti's confidence. If this man who was about to put his hands on her could be turned on to the point of erection, maybe she wasn't a freak. This time she scored an A. She caressed his penis and brought him to orgasm, but when he offered to do the same for her, she demurred. Patti did not want her penis involved. At the end of that class, after Patti had changed back to male drab and just before he walked out the door, he said, "Patricia wants a boyfriend."

After that, Pat explored gay male life. He had two boyfriends for very short periods. "I was trying everything," Patti says. "I didn't really leave any stones unturned."

And I thought, "Eureka!" I was so happy that Pat was finally having sex. I began to envision Pat a gay man and suggested that instead of wearing a wig, he might cut what little hair he had really short, sort of a brunette Noël Coward—long legs and fingers, his hair close cropped, wearing a silk smoking jacket. But that was not Patti's vision. Again, it was that penis that was the sticking point.

She has explained:

Part of the problem with gay relationships for me was that people focused on my masculinity. They focused on my penis, they focused on my build. I was expected to be a guy, and the more they treated me like a guy, especially since at six four I was very big, the worse I felt. Because I wanted to be treated as a woman and I wanted to think of myself as a woman and the idea that someone would value me for my penis was too horrifying. I just couldn't deal with that. So I ended up breaking off those relationships because I wasn't happy. For me that was a dead end. I've always felt that I should be a woman, but I didn't think it was possible. Still, I felt too unhappy to continue existing the way I was.

In February 1995, I was invited by Dr. Vern Bullough to make a presentation before the First International Conference on Gender & Sex at CalState University in Northridge (www.csun.edu/~sr2022). I suggested that Patti and student Jennifer James accompany me to help. I felt they could both benefit from the conference, each in her own way. Patti was so hungry for knowledge, and Jennifer loved being social and being an academy ambassadress. It proved to be a turning point for Pat. It was the first place that he really saw transsexuals, and he learned more about transsexualism in general. "The conference was very inspiring. I learned there was a way that I could be happy, and for the first time I began to believe it. I returned determined that I would disclose my feeling to my mother."

Patti's father, a New York policeman, had died when Pat was thirty-seven, just before he entered the academy. Pat went to see his mother, armed with all of the material from the conference and announced, "I am transsexual."

Patti says, "She asked some basic questions, like how long had I felt this way and was I going to get an operation. Her first reaction, a common one, was guilt. She wanted to know if it was something she had done wrong. She said, 'Well, you seemed like a normal boy.' Had she dropped me on my head? I explained to her that it was not something she'd done, this is just the way I am. There are a lot of theories about what makes people transsexual, but there is not a lot of evidence supporting any one theory. To me, it is just a fact of my life and not something that was caused by an external event. At one point she shrugged and said, 'Oh, it probably comes from your father's side of the family.' "

It was a month before the annual drag charity ball, the Night of 1000 Gowns (www.imperialcourtny.org), so Patti invited her mother to accompany her. It would be Pat's way of introducing his mother to Patricia. They had a fabulous time. "My mother has been very accepting of my transition and supportive, though she is totally mystified."

What's that I hear? Are there some doubting Thomasinas out there who believe you cannot come out to your loved ones because they would never understand? In 1999, an enterprising tranny named Yvonne conducted a survey of visitors to her website. Of the 1,300 cross-dressers who responded, two-thirds were married or in significant relationships, and one-third were divorced or in the process. Of the two-thirds who were married/committed, three-quarters had revealed their cross-dressing to their partners (www.yvonnesplace.net). Patti's mother did not understand, but still she was able to accept and support Patti because she loved her child. Patti helped by being prepared with printed information.

Another chief area of concern is work. "What if my employer finds out?" you ask. Pat came out as a cross-dresser on HBO's *Real Sex*. He could be a bit bolder because he was single, but he was still anxious to know how all this would go over at work. The show was broadcast four or five times during November 1994, and Patti waited for some feedback. Nothing, not a word. It was almost disappointing. Finally, one of Patti's more straightforward colleagues asked him if he'd been on HBO. The man had not seen the show himself, but, he said, "Everyone's talking about it." There was even a tape of the program making the rounds of the hospital. "It really had no impact on my job," Patti said. "I work with a bunch of intelligent people whose chief concern is that I can do the work. I guess they feel what I do in my spare time is private. It was almost as if they found out I was a skier."

Patti's appearance at work began gradually but steadily to change. At first, it was hardly noticeable. He bought himself a flowered pen. He began to wear stud earrings. Then he decided to wear Patricia's nail extensions all the time, and long polished fingernails became Pat's trademark. He packed in the Grateful Dead tees (after all, Jerry Garcia was gone, too). Patti's new favorite shirt had a big yellow sunflower emblazoned across her chest. He let what little hair he had grow long and held it in place with a scrunchee. Patti continued her classes at the academy and nurtured herself in other ways as well. Instead of lifting a few with the neighborhood guys, Patti joined the social whirl that is the Imperial Court of New York, the drag charity organization. She participated in a support group at the Gender Identity Project and regularly saw counselor Carrie Davis at the Lesbian, Gay, Bisexual & Transgender Community Center (www.gaycenter.org) on West 13th Street. Our girl Patti had even become a gender rights activist with the lobby groups GenderPAC (www.gpac.org) and New York Association for Gender Rights Advocacy (www.nyagra.org), whose primary goal is to end the violence and economic discrimination that is directed at transgendered people. It became much easier to refer to her as "Patricia" as well as "Patti." I began referring to Pat as "she" no matter how she was dressed because I understood that in her heart, Pat was female. By 2000 she had made up her mind to make the transition.

The biggest change would be at work because she would be arriving each day in femme mode, a longhaired wig, a dress when she chose, lipstick and makeup, girl's shoes—the works. Patti came to me with a plan. Her department was hosting a millennium party off hospital premises. She reasoned it was the perfect opportunity to introduce everyone to Patricia. "It's at a separate catering hall, so I won't be disturbing work at the hospital. And it's a party, an evening affair, so I can get completely dressed up and present myself in the best possible light."

I marveled at how well she had thought through everything. It must have been her woman's intuition. She planned to tell a few colleagues ahead of time and let the news into the gossip mill, so people would be somewhat prepared.

I was very excited for her and very proud. She was taking such care every step of the way. As Patti said, "It was time." She had been seeing a private therapist and in two months would begin taking hormones. A year after the party she planned to be dressing and living as a woman full-time. She wanted to give her coworkers time to adjust to the idea.

Happily, I was a part of her evening. As the party was on a Monday night, she would be spending the day at work in male attire. We decided that it would be more relaxing for her to have her makeup done by one of our deans, Miss Maria, at the academy. The party was in a luxurious penthouse conveniently located just four blocks from our school.

I decided to videotape her makeover on this momentous occasion. I called the tape the "Patti Project." Miss Maria did an inspired makeup job. Patricia was particularly happy with her lips. "Sometimes I make them too big," she said, "but these are just the right size." She put on her prettiest blue dress, the real swishy one. "It's the one that has had the most flirtatious success." She said, "People seem to come on to me when I am wearing it." Red hair, jewelry, perfume . . . she was a knockout.

I invited her to come back and give me a report at the end of the night. She returned even more aglow.

"When I arrived, the woman who sat at a table taking our tickets looked at me perplexed, obviously not recognizing who I was. Then I passed her the ticket with my name on it. She looked down at my name, then up at my face, then down at my name, then up at my face, and said really loudly, before she could stop herself, 'It's Pat Harrington in drag!' As I checked my coat, I could hear the buzz start. 'It's Pat Harrington in drag! It's Pat Harrington in drag!' People told me I looked great."

One male coworker gave her a kiss on the cheek and told her she was gorgeous. The religious people who she feared might take offense sat right at her table and broke bread with her. As it was a social situation, people had the opportunity to ask her questions, which they sure did. And when her boss, the department chairman, came over to their table to greet everyone he said, "Happy New Year, Patricia." It was respect and recognition from someone whose opinion carried a lot of weight. It was a feather in the chapeau of our blossoming career girl. Patricia was not only courageous, she was glamorous, my favorite combination, and she was aware of her power. She understood that because she entered the room full of confidence, looking her best, a smile on her face, sure of who she was and not afraid to face those who might not agree, people were drawn to her. She had helped direct their reactions and treated them with care, just as she wanted to be treated. Patti had cleared the way for herself.

After three months in private therapy, Patricia's therapist wrote a letter attesting to her delicate condition. Never was a person more pleased to be certifiable. The letter was required before she could proceed to the next step, hormones.

Patti planned to begin taking hormones at the beginning of 2000. Coincidentally, in February a British film crew was scheduled to shoot what has since become *The Tranny School,* the one-hour documentary about the academy. Perfect timing. They could document Patti's first swallow.

I bought a bottle of champagne for the occasion. "These are Premarin," she informed me. "They are made from the urine of pregnant mares." I offered a toast, "To you, Patricia." She lifted the tiny pill to her eager lips, fumbling a bit, what with her long nails and her excitement. "Well, here goes!" Down went the horse piss followed by champagne—pink, of course. It was her birthday.

The Transition

As a tranny, you may consider yourself very self-sufficient. You may have kept your femmeself very private. But if you plan to transition from male to female, it's time to go beyond the do-it-yourself method. The guidelines for transition are the Standards of Care as formulated by the Harry Benjamin Gender Dysphoria Association (HBIGDA) (www.hbigda.org), which those in the know pronounce "habigda." In 1966 Dr. Harry Benjamin authored *The Transexual Phenomenon,* the seminal work on the subject (www.symposion.com/ijt/benjamin). In short form, these are the guidelines:

1. Real-life experience in the preferred gender role, at least one year.
2. Hormone therapy.
3. Surgery to change genitalia and other sex characteristics.

If you are serious about transitioning, or even simply curious, a visit to the website of Dr. Anne Lawrence and the Transsexual Women's Resources (www.annelawrence.com/twr) is a must. Here you will find links to HBIGDA, personal accounts of people's surgeries, a sort of consumer reports of orchiectomies (castration); sex-reassignment surgeries; facial feminizations; and more, including photos from doctors displaying their talents: new breasts, vulvas, penises (for women to men).

We've come a long way in the few short years since 1956 when Christine Jorgensen's sex-reassignment surgery shocked the world.

A word of caution to you eager beavers who may be popping pills with no medical supervision. Hormones are drugs and very powerful ones. They can affect your body in many ways, some of which, such as forming breast tissue, can be irreversible. Hormones are available on the black market, but that is one place where I advise you not to shop. Stealing your sister's birth control pills is a definite no-no. That's carrying Venus envy to dangerous lengths. You might find yourself an uncle long before you are ever called auntie, not to mention the havoc you could wreak in other people's lives. If you have been taking hormones unsupervised, don't be afraid to go to a doctor and 'fess up. Dr. Lawrence, for instance, and other doctors are flexible about these matters, believing that, even if you have not spent a year in therapy or a year in your preferred role, if you are going to take hormones anyway, it is better to let you continue taking them under a doctor's supervision than to leave you out in the cold.

Patti plans to enjoy every step of her transition and won't rush into any gender reassignment surgery. Surgeons' fees vary: $6,000 at present in Thailand, $10,000 in Canada, and up to $26,000 in the United States. Except in cases of city workers in San Francisco, these fees are not yet covered by health insurance plans. The website called Financing Transition for Transsexual

Women (www.tsroadmap.com/reality/finance) offers practical advice on these and other money matters. Some factors Patricia considers important are location, experience, and price. If she travels to Thailand, she could get more of a bargain, but it would be a long way to travel should there be any postsurgery complications. A U.S. surgeon would be quite handy but more expensive. A doctor with lots of experience sounds ideal, but what if she feels like she is on an assembly line?

Surgeons make presentations at the different gender conferences and conventions that take place each year, another advantage of being involved in the tranny network. You can shop before you chop.

Jennifer James gets ready for school.
(Photo by Annie Sprinkle)

CHAPTER 13

Discipline Problems

*A*s a student at the academy, when you go out and about town, you are always accompanied by two deans. Aside from a threesome being more fun, I believe there's safety in numbers. You present a united front, a trio of amazons, breasts lifted and proud. The deans have had more experience as femmes fatales than you, who may very well be a debutante, out for the very first time. They are quick to spot trouble before it starts. Let's face it, there are a lot of villains out there who think it is perfectly fine to harass women and who will be quite happy to harass you. There comes a time when every bird has to leave the nest and fly solo, and you have to watch out for those birds of prey.

When Patti Harrington's job took her to Paris, she decided to spend some of her time out and about en femme.

Patti in Paris

I went to Montmartre to get a reservation for the show at the famous drag club Chez Michou (www .michou.fr). I did not know that this club was right around the corner from the rue Pigalle, which is the red-light district of Paris, and this particular street happened to be the tranny stroll. As I was going down the hill, one of these aggressive fellows came up to me and started a conversation. I tried to say *"Je ne parle pas français"* (I don't speak French). So he put his thumb in his mouth and began sliding it in and out, then asking, *"Comprenez-vous? Comprenez-vous?"* It was apparent that he wanted a blow job. He's asking *"Combien? Combien? Trois cent francs? Trois cent francs?"* He wanted to pay me three hundred francs [about $60 at the time] to blow him. Naturally, I freaked out. This was totally beyond my experience. I hurried away and he ran after me yelling, *"Cinq cent francs, cinq cent francs!"* [$100], waving five bills in his hand. I really panicked, thinking I could be arrested for prostitution. It was so blatant. So I jumped in the subway and headed back to my hotel. En route, I had to walk through a long tunnel in order to change trains. Two guys stood drinking something out of paper bags. As I walked by, they said something. I had no clue what they were saying and I was scared. One of them put his hand up my skirt. I was stone still with panic like a deer caught in the headlights. I gritted my teeth and thought, "This is it. He's going to grab me and squeeze, and it's going to hurt." Instead, he caressed me and, though I was totally scared, I was turned on. He said something to his friend that I didn't understand, then he put his hand up my skirt again and continued caressing my crotch. I turned and ran. The train pulled in the station just then, so I jumped on board.

Patti explained to me that she had ambivalent feelings in this situation. She knew that she was being harassed, but there was a part of her that took it as a compliment and a turn-on. She reacted the way a child does, with confusion. She had only recently discovered her sexuality. My advice to her and to others of you in similar situations is to stand up for yourself, observe the warning signs, and put such predators in their places. No matter how happy you are that someone seems to be attracted to you, don't fall for it. You deserve better. Someone who is too forward is not looking to make you happy. He is looking to take advantage of you for his own amusement, gratification, or sense of power. Please remember that your actions have consequences for you and for the next girl.

Stay on Your Toes

What do you do when you are being harassed? An ounce of prevention is worth a pound of cure. Learn to recognize the MO. Strangers who ask personal questions in inappropriate situations are looking for an opening. If that taxi driver asks you if you are married, ignore him. Or simply say, "Sir, that is really not your business." I love the "sir" technique. I learned it from my bosom buddy Veronica Hart, one of the great porn stars, now as Jane Hamilton a very respected adult-film director/producer. Jane had made a lot of sexy movies and she never knew when she might be recognized by someone who might have some preconceived notions about how familiar he could get with her. The first time I heard her address a stranger as "sir" I noticed how it immediately put him on his best behavior, demanded of him a reciprocal distance and politeness. I've used it ever since. The more you go out and about, the more you will face challenges. Like any tests they are easier when you are prepared. You can be a slut in private, you can be a slut at an orgy, you can even feel you are a slut in your heart of hearts, but you are still entitled to be treated as a lady, so don't relinquish your rights.

How do you deal with a *frotteur*? (Thought I'd include a bit of erotic vocabulary lesson.) A *frotteur* is a "rubber," a person who rubs up against you in a crowded place like a subway car or elevator. These men can be very persistent. My advice is to ask him loud and clear, "What do you think you are doing?" This same technique can be applied to the horny man who catches your attention by rubbing his penis. These men are subjecting you to sexual abuse, not admiration. When confronted they usually shrivel up like the worms that they are.

Actions speak louder than words, and it is good to be prepared. Take physical self-defense classes—women take them all the time. In Manhattan, they are taught at the Gay & Lesbian Center among many other places. Actually, it might be a great way to meet somebody. All sweated up, being physically close, feeling the chemistry, getting to know each other, taking it slow, week after week, hold after hold . . . but I digress. You don't have to become a black belt, though that's not a bad idea. But it is a great and empowering thing to know some basic moves for disabling an attacker. A good kick in the groin is a time-honored response. Remember, if you are going to run, don't trip over your heels: either take off your pumps or run on your toes.

If a crime is committed against you, report it to the police. You may be afraid to go to the police, and with good cause. The police have not always given equal treatment to trannies. "It's that old blame-the-victim prejudice, though the situation is improving as more and more trannies come out, even tranny police. And you have advocates. In New York (www.avp.org) and at least twenty other major cities, there are gay and lesbian and transgender antiviolence projects. Let your first call be to them.

The Mouths of Babes

Have you got the time? The more you stroll about, the more you may notice that people are very interested in the time. They see you coming; they are not sure if you are male or female, so they want to hear your voice. Let your instincts guide you. If the question comes from a rowdy group of teenagers, chances are you might want to avoid them. Just hold your head high and walk on by quickly. If you don't feel threatened you might want to smile and answer, letting the person know what time it is in more than one sense. Without saying the words you'll be letting him or her know: "What time is it? It's tranny time. Get used to it."

How do you set limits without being a party pooper? Let's face it, girls, people are curious and right now is an interesting time for trannies. People know just enough to be aware of the phenomenon but not enough to know rules of behavior. It is your job to teach them. Suppose you are at a party and someone admires your sweater and then asks you how you stuff your bra. You might not want to answer that question. Just tell her you find that question "a bit too personal, dear." Then again, you may be very proud of how you have sculpted your body, and you might want to brag: "A stocking filled with two pounds of bird seed in each." Just know that you have a choice.

What if the awkward question comes from a child? Let me tell you how Miss Viqui answered her four-year-old son Taylor's questions about Patti Harrington. Patricia, one of Taylor's godparents, has known him since he was born. One day Taylor, who knew Pat and now was seeing Patricia blossom, asked his mother if Patti was a man or a woman. Viqui answered, "Patti was a man who is becoming a woman." The answer was accurate and seemed to be satisfactory, at least for a while. On another occasion, Patti and I were visiting Viqui when Taylor and his neighbor Emma, a seven-year-old girl, entered. Obviously, the kids have had little chats among themselves about Patti because as soon as Emma saw Patti she greeted her with, "Do you have a penis?" She took all of the adults by surprise and we laughed. Emma looked very proud of herself for having been the source of our amusement. Then we all caught ourselves and her mother took her aside and reminded her not to ask personal questions and certainly not in a room full of people. I thought about it and realized we had all made a mistake. We had confused her. Our laughter said one thing; our words said another. And laughter is very powerful. If we wanted to teach her appropriate behavior, we must not reward inappropriate behavior with laughter, making her the star of the show, especially when the joke is at someone else's expense. Just recently, Viqui and her husband, John, were discussing babies. Taylor asked a question and, not really wanting to include him in the conversation, they chose to ignore it. "I guess I'll just wait till I grow up and then I'll become a woman and have a baby and then I'll know." Just for emphasis he added, "Patti's doing it."

John said, "You could become a woman, but you would not be able to have a baby."

At least, not yet, but who knows! Thank goodness for the questions of children. They really keep us on our toes. Our future depends on how we answer them.

As a tranny, you are helping to make the world a better place. The mere fact of your existence puts out a call for tolerance. It helps us all to understand that there is much more to the variety of human existence and experience than simply a) woman and b) man. Variety enriches the world. Unfortunately, not everyone heeds the call or, rather, their response to that call is fear, bigotry, and violence. Since the academy's inception, I have always been careful to state we are not into corporal punishment. No spanking permitted, no matter how much you beg for it. I've put a funny spin on it, but violence, even spanking, is no joke. As you may understand only too well, children have been spanked too often just for being who they are. Tranny kids have been among those who are physically or psychologically abused to the point they feel they must run away to grow. Sometimes they are cast out or thrown away. I am not saying that every child—even every tranny child who runs away—has been abused, because that is not so. But this lesson is about tranny bashing, sexual harassment, and violence—and, sadly, childhood is often where it starts.

I am in awe of the determination of children to be who they are. Boy George, in his autobiography, *Take It Like a Man,* describes how he was put down and pushed around just for being different. He developed sissy power, and it helped fuel his creativity. But not every abused tranny winds up a superstar.

Here is a letter I received from a prisoner.

I am thirty-four years old but I would like to be referred to as Chelsea Nicole who is currently only six years old. . . . I have always felt inside that I should have been born as a girl, but because I had parents who abused me sexually, physically, and emotionally I was forced to hide my feelings deep inside for thirty-one years. But it was not until the age of thirty-three and with the help of therapy in prison that I began to realize these feelings still existed. Now all the feelings that I had stuffed deep inside all these years are pouring out uncontrollably and they are that of a six-year-old little girl. This little girl is who I feel I am today and want so desperately to become that it hurts and even makes me break out in tears.

Miss Vera, as a child and as an adult, I have never yet had the opportunity to experience my feminine side. I have never been able to dress up as a little girl and it is something I feel very strongly about wanting to do, because it is who I feel I am. I even find myself having feelings of a little girl about wanting to be loved, held, and cared for. I feel as if I have missed out on my entire childhood because I had to hide who I really was for my own protection as a child. . . . Miss Vera, will you please teach me what I need to know about being a little girl and also help me to have the childhood I never had?

Yours truly,
Chelsea Nicole

Was this convict playing on my heartstrings to con me into being a pen pal? I asked Chelsea what he was in for, but he would not tell me. He had been in prison for many years. Maybe it was all true. Maybe violence had begat violence and he had hurt others. I could give Chelsea a pretty dress to wear, but I could not give him back his childhood. I wish I could.

Trannies who have died violently are memorialized at the site called Remembering Our Dead (www.gender.org/remember). Brave trannies were in the front lines of the rebellion at the Stonewall Inn, which is heralded as the start of the Gay Pride—now named Gay/Lesbian/Bi/Transgender—movement. Tranny kids are organizing now. A link from www.annelawrence.com brings you to Sarah's Room. Sarah, now twenty, began her site as a teenager. It is large and informative, with links to the personal pages of other transgendered teens throughout the United States. They are not waiting for permission to be, they just are. Bless the children.

Gayle and Hank enjoy their wedding dance.
(Photo by Nancy Rica Schiff)

CHAPTER 14

Always a Bride

I call Gayle our perennial bride because each of her visits has involved a bridal gown. Gayle is the femmeself of Cameron, a sixty-year-old entrepreneur and Southern belle who for the past three years takes a few days out of his life to spend with us as Gayle. No one knows about Gayle, not Cameron's wife (who takes a separate vacation) or his grandchildren or any of his business colleagues or friends. Gayle is Cameron's secret and as much as he might like to be open about Gayle, Cameron likes his secret. Once he arrives at the academy, Cameron disappears and Gayle emerges. On her first visit, Gayle brought her own wedding dress that Cameron had purchased online from David's Bridal. It was a lovely, full-skirted creation with a chapel-length train, short sleeves, and a sweetheart neckline (Gayle's favorite style), and it was embellished with beaded lace. It was also about two sizes too large because, after he bought the gown, as a prelude to Gayle's academy visit, Cameron had gone on a diet. He was not the first academy student who, either before or after enrollment, was inspired to make the girl in the mirror conform to the vision in his mind's eye. Immediately after Gayle's emergence that first day of her very first femme intensive, we made an unscheduled visit to Miss Maria Christina, dressmaker par excellence, for emergency dress surgery. Fortunately, she was able to accomplish the task in the day and a half remaining before Gayle's bridal photo shoot. While the dressmaker worked to make Gayle's gown picture-perfect, I introduced Gayle to the faculty who would guide her in her lessons: walking with Miss Maryanne, voice with Miss Judy, makeup with Miss Deborah and Miss Maria, etiquette with Miss Melissa, and principles of seduction with Miss Eva. The too tall blondes, Miss Kate and Miss Barbara, took her under their wings for an afternoon shopping spree. A highlight of this first academy visit was the photo shoot by Mariette Pathy Allen.

It was a splendid fall day, the leaves had turned amber, and we used Mother Nature as a backdrop for Gayle's wedding pictures that Mariette shot in Riverside Park. Miss Melissa, our petite dean of etiquette, carried Gayle's train and was dwarfed by our six-foot-two bride. Imagine (and I am sure you can) the thrill Gayle experienced as she took those first steps out in her lovely bridal gown. Cameron had been very discreet and private these past sixty years, never wanting to upset the security of his life and loved ones. The thought that he might hurt someone, especially his wife, brought tears to his eyes, but he did not want to be sitting in a rocking chair one day, regretting that he had never permitted himself this experience. It took Cameron several years from the time he first read my book to actually contact the academy. Until then, he had kept his bridal gown in a storage locker, taking it out when opportunities arose for him to dress and sit alone in his finery, like Miss Havisham awaiting the groom who never came. During that first visit, Gayle dropped a number of hints to let me know that she was longing for a groom. Her evening bag held a supply of condoms and when I asked her how she had enjoyed her canopied bed at the Inn on 23rd Street, she told me that she was only sorry she had to sleep in it alone. All of which led me to the conclusion that as part of her class in experiencing her female sexual energy, Gayle might enjoy a trip to the masseur. I was right. Hank the masseur did a laying on of hands that was so transformative our debutante might have been with a faith healer. In a way, she was. I observed discreetly and made careful watch from an adjoining room. At one point, Gayle sighed and said, "This is what I have been waiting for all my life." She was a much more relaxed person when we left the massage studio. City traffic had held us up and made us a bit behind schedule. To save time, Gayle suggested she remain in her same dress for dinner.

A tranny who does not want to change her clothes . . . it's a miracle what a good shag can do.

One year later, on her second visit to the academy, Gayle asked to go shopping for another bridal gown. So Gayle, Miss Maria, and I planned a field trip to David's Bridal Salon in Brooklyn. I telephoned ahead and explained to the store manager the exact nature of Miss Vera's Finishing School. She was very accommodating and even permitted us to bring Mariette along to photograph Gayle's try-ons. Being in the bridal salon, sorting through rows and rows of white wedding dresses, was like being lost inside a vat of very heavy whipped cream, though I am sure you would not mind taking a plunge. A girl could really work up a sweat lifting some of those frocks. Gayle found a gown that fit her very specific requirements, a long-sleeved sheath with a sweetheart neckline. It was covered with lace and trimmed with tiny pearls. The dress had a court train, which meant it was fine for twirling but not so long as to be treacherous. Only one alteration was needed. The gown was designed with thirty buttons down the back, which would be fine for a bride with attendants, but for those times—and there would be many—when Gayle would not have help, she needed to dress herself. So we waited just an hour while a store seamstress changed the buttons for a zipper. Gayle put the time to good use trying on gowns from the bridesmaid's department. So many dresses, so little time! We held a bridal shower at the academy with the deans and student Patricia participating. Gayle even let Patricia try on her new gown. Knowing how much Gayle loved her new dress, I was surprised at her sisterly generosity. When she had visited us for the first time a year before, she had been more controlling and felt the need to question me each step of the way. Once Gayle learned she could trust us and have a good time, she wanted to be sure others did too. She also found time to rendezvous with the masseur with the healing hands. Gayle had asked me to arrange her reunion with Hank, but I told her no and explained why. "It's one thing for me to lead you to an experience that helps you to learn more about yourself. After that, you need to take responsibility for your choices." I wasn't going to set Gayle up with dates. But it was not "dates" on which she had her heart set. Gayle was an old-fashioned romantic from the Liz Taylor school of courtship. She was out to land a husband.

By Gayle's third visit, she was ready for a wedding. To one extent she was a modern girl. She had proposed to Hank and he was up for it. Hank was a delightful, talented man with a very good sense of humor. His massage practice supplemented his income as a college professor and helped finance his career as a painter. It also expanded his sex life in ways that he found very fulfilling. Hank enjoyed being naked, being appreciated for his body and for his sexual prowess. He was quite happy to costar in Gayle's wet dream. The rest of the details were left to me. The wedding would be a fantasy come true. It was a big responsibility, but I was fortunate to have my experience as a fairy godmother and the academy deans to help me. There was a steady stream of challenges and I soared above these hurdles like a Thoroughbred.

With the who, what, and when lined up, there remained only the where. Since its opening in 1999, I had recommended the Inn on 23rd Bed and Breakfast to our out-of-town students. The innkeepers, Annette and Barry, have made it a place of warmth and charm, the perfect resting place for Miss Vera's sleeping beauties. Each room is decorated in the style of a particular era. There are vanity tables from the forties, and fifties chairs upholstered in zebra-print fabric, and crystal chandeliers no matter what the decade. My favorites are the rooms in which the beds are veiled in gossamer canopies. Throughout, Annette has hung their family photos, which add still more to the welcoming atmosphere. There is a spacious library on the second floor that is just the right size for about thirty wedding guests. Since Gayle was staying at the inn, it was very convenient. We could hire another room for bridesmaids to dress and it would be as if our bride were having her wedding in her own home.

Gayle began to call me regularly with questions and ideas. Your anticipation of a visit to our academy is part of the fun. This was the role Gayle was born to play and she was playing it to the hilt. "I would love Patti to be my maid of honor," she said. Academy graduate Patricia Harrington was enthused. She and Gayle had met only once, and their motives for attending the academy were different. Gayle was happy to return to her life as Cameron. Patricia (or Patti, we used the names interchangeably now) planned to change her life forever. She was a year into her transition from male to female and the idea of being a maid of honor supported her in becoming the woman she felt herself to be. A wedding is a powerful ritual that can touch the hearts of those who participate in many different ways. It was Patricia who suggested Mikeli Capozzi officiate the ceremony. Having Mikeli officiate would set just the right tone. Mikeli has been my friend for a dozen years, almost since his arrival from Genoa. He refers to himself as an "urban explorer" and "pornologist." When not conducting tours of Harlem and of New York's underground sex scene, he produces adult movies. He would be a sort of a kinky Father Guido Sarducci.

It was Indian summer, but Gayle could not resist ordering a platinum faux-fox jacket from Fabulous Furs (www.fabulousfurs.com).

With the aid of the Internet, ordering two reasonably priced gold wedding bands, size 11, was a cinch. I had a nice chat with Judy at Houston Jewelers (www.weddingringsuperstore.com), who oversaw the order and the engraving.

But first was the near catastrophe of Gayle's dress. Before she left home, Gayle informed me that she had tried on her gown and it was small across the back. "Bring a second," I said, remembering she had another and that it was larger. But did Gayle listen to her teacher? No. She really wanted to wear the pearl sheath, and, as hope springs eternal in a tranny's breast, she preferred to think that the dress could be altered to fit. Gayle arrived in New York, and we began the hectic first day with preparations. The plans included makeover, nail extensions at Beauty & Youth Salon, final dress fitting, and new hair, all under the tutelage of Miss Deborah, dean of cosmetology, and Miss Melissa, dean of etiquette. Then a movie date in the evening with her fiancé. I welcomed Gayle, entrusted her to the deans, and then went to my inner sanctum to continue organizing the weekend. I was not long at my desk when I got an emergency call. The trio was at the dressmaker's and the news was not good. The gown was way too small and the dressmaker, Maria Christina, informed me she could not accomplish the extensive alterations in time for the wedding two days hence. She said if I got the same gown two sizes larger, she could make that work in time.

This was a job for the tranny goddess. I felt an adrenaline rush as I let my fingers fly into action. Being a Scorpio, I am a born investigator. I took out the Yellow Pages and let my fingers do some walking. David's Bridal did not have the gown in the next size. Finally, I found Rosa's Bridal Salon. The dressmaker informed me that all dresses were custom-made. After telling her our wedding was two days hence, I was about to hang up when she asked me our specific requirements. "I have a size twenty-two right here," she said. "Yes, it is a sheath. The neckline is sweetheart and there is a train." This was too good to be true and only fifteen blocks away. I tracked down the academy trio by phone and told them to meet me at Rosa's.

Rosa's Bridal Salon was located at the back of Hamed Fabrics in the heart of New York's garment center on West 39th Street. There were a couple of Pakistani fellows at the front counter and a pair of African women dressed in dashikis and turbans splashed with color. They carried babies on their backs as they shopped the rows and rows of bolts. It reminded me of my visit to Nairobi. A radio blared what sounded like Arabic music. I imagined Gayle's reaction when she saw this place. She is a genteel girl from a very white-bread environment. The atmosphere at Hamed's was foreign and exotic. There were more people of color in the store that day than she probably saw in a year at home. I must admit that I felt a devilish glee in what I suspected might be a challenge to Gayle's composure. Had she heeded my suggestion and brought that second dress, she would not be in this predicament. Remember, Miss Vera knows best!

Fortunately, the environment in Rosa's Bridal Salon on the

mezzanine was perfectly pink and reassuring. At the center of the space was a mirrored dressing table trimmed with a lace skirt and festooned with pink tulle and plastic roses. One mannequin held a ball gown made from what looked like spun gold fit for a fairy-tale princess. It had poufy elbow-length sleeves and a full skirt. On another mannequin was a form-fitting chiffon evening gown held up by diamanté-laden spaghetti straps. Rows of glass show-cases held tiaras made from sequins, rhinestones, and pearls—all of them just waiting for veils to be attached. Behind one of the counters sat Rosa, busy at her sewing table, yards of white lace draped over her lap. Behind another counter two men were hav-ing a conversation in a language I did not recognize.

I introduced myself to Rosa, and she showed me the gown she had in mind. It was more satin than lace, but it was a long-sleeved sheath as advertised. The neck was not sweetheart style. "I can change the neckline," Rosa said confidently. Moments later my cell phone rang with Melissa checking in. "I think it is worth a trip up here," I told her. To Rosa I suggested that when the bride to be arrived, the two chatty gentlemen make themselves scarce. We didn't need them as a reception committee. Poof, they were gone. I sat in a pretty little upholstered chair from which I had a good view of the shop's front door. As soon as I saw them I waved a reassuring hand and directed them through Hamed's jungle of fabric up to the mezzanine that hung above like a fluffy piece of heaven.

When Gayle spotted the other dress, she began to sniff dis-approval. "It doesn't have a sweetheart neck," she said as we stripped her down to her corset and undies. As far as I and Miss Deborah and Miss Melissa were concerned, there was no way she was not going to at least try it on. Gayle made a hands-first bridal dive into the dress (a move she had been taught at David's Bridal) and did not protest. Let's face it, would you? As Rosa, the nimble-fingered dressmaker, assured us she could make all kinds of changes, Miss Deborah asked if she could alter Gayle's own gown in time to fit.

"Something told me to bring this dress," said Miss Deborah (bless her!) as she and Miss Melissa toted the extra-long garment bag across the room for Gayle to do another dive.

Talk about transformations . . . as soon as the dressmaker announced that she could alter the gown we had brought in time for Gayle to wear it down the aisle, our anxious bride began to purr like a pussycat. Her fears calmed, she took a more open-minded view of her surroundings. In the wink of a false eyelash, she spotted a cathedral-length veil and began to search the showcases for a tiara. Miss Deborah, who was way ahead of her, had already made a few selections.

In case you have not already realized it, the deans of the academy are very versatile. Each is an expert in her particular field but also knows how to adapt to many situations. Our dean of cosmetology, Miss Deborah, is a shopping maven. She has a great eye and understands what will look terrific on you. Plus she is delighted to go shopping with other people's money. Gayle trusted Miss Deb's fashion sense and needed no coaxing to loosen her purse strings, especially when wedding accessories were involved. By the time we left, Gayle's dress, her new cathedral veil, and bejeweled tiara—along with a lace-trimmed pillow for the ring bearer—were all sewed up.

A camera is an important tranny tool, second only to a mirror. As is our custom, we took lots of photos at the bridal salon and we were still on schedule for Gayle's appointment at Barry Hendricksen's Bitz N Pieces wig boutique.

Does it surprise you to learn that our bride was a blonde? I think not. Gayle is tall and Nordic, like Britt Ekland or Julie Newmar. She went shopping with real hair on her mind, but I told her to make a lace-cap wig her top priority. A lace-cap wig gives the appearance that hair is growing right out of your scalp, which is really the effect that you want. Performers use them all the time, as evidenced by the black-and-white glossies of Madonna, RuPaul, Diana Ross, and others that line this salon's walls. This time Gayle heeded her teacher's advice. The stylist at Bitz N Pieces was so expert, everyone agreed the very first wig she put on Gayle's head was perfection, but, of course, Gayle needed to try on quite a number to be sure. The goal is the journey. Gayle's lace-cap acrylic 'do cost $750. A similar wig made from human hair carried a higher price tag ($1,800) and was tempting, but I was happy that our bride exercised restraint. Why gild a lily?

That evening Gayle spent with her swain. All restrictions on the groom seeing the bride before the wedding did not apply. It was not as if these two would actually be spending the rest of their lives together. No, these few days were stolen moments in Cameron's secret life as Gayle. Gayle brought with her a generous dowry that took care of, among other things, the bills for their dinner dates and nights on the town. Hank's rewards were tangible, but he was also caught up in the fantasy much as a gay actor might be when he plays a straight romeo. On the one hand, Cameron and Hank were gay, but they were living as a straight couple, so they were also not gay. I know it sounds complicated, and it is. Sexual orientation is far more complex and varied than we have presumed so far, and no one knows that better than all of us at Miss Vera's. Hank enjoyed being a heartthrob and he definitely enjoyed being a stud. He was even inspired to change his last name to Hardman, though it was too late to revise the wedding invitations.

Every bride needs some bridesmaids. What could be more appropriate than inviting some tranny bridesmaids. I contacted Caprice Bellefleur, a bespectacled male accountant by day who doffs his three-piece suit to be a disco dolly in a party dress at night. Caprice was a member of Cross-Dresser's International (CDI), the local support group. I invited Caprice to participate in the wedding. "If you know other girls with something extra who might like to come, please feel free to invite one or two. Be sure these are trannies who understand that it is not them but the bride who must be in the spotlight." Caprice caught my drift.

"I'll have to make arrangements with my wife," Caprice explained. The wedding would take place on a Friday evening. "My deal with her is that I can be Caprice during the week, but not on weekends. Friday is kind of a gray area, so I think, as long as I catch her in a good mood, I won't have a problem being a bridesmaid." Like some couples, Caprice and his wife have learned to compromise regarding cross-dressing.

Patti Harrington, our maid of honor, had invited her friend Countess Ashley Pennington, a member of the Imperial Court of New York, the charity organization whose motto is "Do Good and Look Fabulous." Ashley takes things like pomp and ceremony quite seriously. She knows how to walk in a procession. So I invited her to be an attendant too.

We had a tranny bride, tranny maid of honor, and two tranny bridesmaids, though I thought I might turn Caprice, who is petite, into a flower girl.

"Miss Vera, who is going to be our best man? It would be fun to have a woman." It was Gayle calling me from home, so excited at the prospect of her upcoming nuptials. Hank, like many a groom, took a backseat in all of these wedding preparations and had even left the choice of best man up to me. I gave Gayle a "we'll see" and made no promises. I had a few zillion other things on my mind. After all, I was mother *and* father of the bride. Little did I know that fate was working things out behind the scenes.

A few months before I had received a call from a lesbian named Tracy who, after watching *The Tranny School,* asked me if she could come to class. She was not the first woman who asked if she could attend. Tracy said she identified with the students. She had recently lost ninety pounds and wanted to explore who she was in her new body. For one thing, she wanted to learn how to walk all over again. I asked her about her sex life and she said she really did not have one, and she was definitely interested in changing that situation. She lived on Long Island and seemed very isolated, so I invited her to come to the wedding and have some fun. She arrived in a suit and tie. Enter the best man.

The day before Gayle's wedding, the deans and I treated her to a bachelorette tea party. I ordered some appropriate items from my friend Helen Wolf's Come Again Erotic Emporium on East 53rd Street: a pair of split-crotch white-lace panties and a corsage made up of tiny penises that glowed in the dark. The highlight of the party occurred when a lady from an adjoining table came over to admire Gayle's ring. Gayle thrust out her newly manicured hand with Chinese-red nail extensions and the five-karat cubic zirconium bauble and accepted compliments and best wishes, while I snapped a photo for the scrapbook.

We ended the afternoon discussing the ceremony with the not-so-officially ordained Fr. Mikeli.

Much to my surprise, Gayle had written the perfect text.

The next day, I walked Gayle down the aisle to give her away. I saw the smiling faces of all in attendance. The innkeepers had come, my friends Candida Royalle (who was destined to catch the bouquet), Amy Rosemarin from the Sex Muse project (www .sexmuse.net), the academy deans, and more. Everyone was smiling and I even saw a few tears. Weddings have that effect on people. And they have a big effect on trannies, especially when it's a transvestite bride.

When it came time for her to speak, Gayle recited the vows she had written.

"I, Gayle, take you, Hank, as my loving husband, to have and to hold, in softness and in hardness, to fondle and caress, to suck and to swallow, and to gaily receive the fullness of your love. I will love, honor, and obey you with heart, mind, and body. My femininity will be submissive to your masculinity. I will lovingly receive your male love and my feminine reward will be your fertile seed. These promises I make and pledge to keep for as long as we both shall cum."

Immediately following the "I do"s Miss Tiger led the happy couple in a symbolic dance. Earlier in the week, my hairdresser Allen Starr had volunteered to be our wedding singer. Hank took Gayle in his arms and thanks to her lessons in dancing backward with Miss Maryanne, our girl let her groom lead to the strains of their wedding song, appropriately titled "We've Only Just Begun." And they had.

Gayle was far from a feminist, but she was definitely liberated. She has by no means graduated from the academy. Her lessons and her journey continue, as I hope will yours, my dear student.

Cherchez la femme, Miss Vera

Miss Vera and Miss Deborah with "Mary Jane." This could be you! (Photo by Mariette Pathy Allen)

Miss Vera's

Resource Guide for Boys
Who Want to Be Girls

Boys who want to be girls can find support all over the world; here I've focused on American sources. There are so many sources, I could not hope to list all of the good ones. I am sure I've left out some that you would deem worthy to be included, but I guarantee, if you start in one place, you will eventually find your way to that other. Many of these items have already been mentioned in the text; in those cases, I may make fewer comments here. Have fun in your research!

Accessories

Ellen Christine Millinery   (www.ellenchristine.com) Ellen says, "Remember to measure across the crown of your head as well as around it for a proper fit and, of course, wear your hair." Small and lovely retail store, 255 W. 18th St., New York, NY, 212-242-2457.

Great Lookz (http://greatlookz.zoovy.com) Accessories galore: white lace-trimmed ankle socks, gloves, hats, scarves, etc.

La Crascia Gloves (www.wegloveyou.com) Glove-cutter Jay will custom fit you. Shop, 304 Fifth Ave., New York, NY, 212-695-0347.

Mimi ala Mode (www.mimialamode.com) Whimsical shower caps.

Spa Turbans (www.spaturban.com) For glamour in the bath.

Artists and Entertainers

Boy George (www.boy.george.net) Not exactly a girl, not exactly a boy—and that is the point. A karma chameleon.

David de Alba's Theatrical Arts & Tributes (http://members.tgforum.com/dealba2/entrance.htm) This site is a treasure trove of information, tributes, and interviews with many of the great modern female impersonators. It is a labor of love from tranny artist David de Alba, who starred at the famed Finocchio's Club in San Francisco until it closed in 1999.

Diva Las Vegas (www.geekbabe.com/dlv/) This informal gathering of cross-dressers has been held for the past five years; it even has its own golf tournament, the DLV open. Participants are encouraged to mix with the public, then meet for specific events.

Eddie Izzard (www.izzard.com) A heterosexual tranny and multi-talented entertainer with a quick tongue.

Frank Marino (www.frankmarino.com) The premiere female impersonator in the country, Frank as Joan Rivers headlines the La Cage review at the Riviera Hotel in Las Vegas. Frank has also written a highly entertaining autobiography, *His Majesty, the Queen,* coauthored with Steve and Cathy Marks. Among other things, the book illustrates Frank's determination to raise the average standard of the drag scene, and I'd say he made it a gold standard. He also discusses his early days, sneaking into his sister's closet. Now he's got huge walk-ins and the doors are wide open.

GenderTalk Radio (www.gendertalk.com) News and interviews. Hosted by the brilliant and sexy team of Nancy Nangeroni and Gordene MacKenzie. Nancy is past president of IFGE and a subject of the A&E *Investigative Report*'s documentary *The Transgender Revolution,* but that only begins to list her areas of activism and accomplishments. Nancy's partner, Gordene, is an award-winning feminist professor and gender activist. Nancy started this program in 1995. It is a great way to stay entertained and informed.

Glorya Wholesome (www.glowgirl.com) Miss Glorya's beauty goes more than skin deep. She is very community oriented. Her site not only tells all about her talented self, but also lets you know what's happening at Trannie Chasers, the club she runs at Nowbar on Seventh Ave. South in New York City.

Hedda Lettuce (www.hedda.com) A drag comedienne who performs regularly at New York's Caroline's Comedy Club, East of Eighth Restaurant, and wherever her witty self is suitably compensated. Great dish on her website.

Hedwig & the Angry Inch (www.hedwigmovie.com) When the stage show ran in New York, it was one of our very favorite academy field trips. Students loved it. We saw it starring its creator, John Cameron Mitchell. We saw it as a GenderPac benefit starring Ally Sheedy. We love the movie. Now *Hedwig* is back in New York and Los Angeles in midnight screenings. This website for the movie gives news of midnight screenings in your town. You can hear the music and you can discover your own glam rock name. Mine came out "Gilded Crotch." Hmmm, sounds very propitious.

Hedwig in a Box (www.hedwiginabox.com) At this fan site you can learn about other Hedwig performers, get all the lyrics to those great songs, plus join the fan club and get updates. Isn't it nice to know you can always "get some Hed"?

Imperial Court of New York (www.imperialcourtny.org) The realm of the Imperial Court includes courts across North America, but New York boasts the most courtiers and courtesans. The major event each year is the Night of 1000 Gowns, a charity drag gala and coronation, held at the Marriott Marquis in early spring and attended by nine hundred people. But these girls raise money for charity all year long and they can help your charity raise money too. Chapters in other states are listed at the site.

International Chrysis (www.wigtech.com/chrysis_page.html) Legendary New York performer (1951–90), now drag angel. She lit up the world for too short a time. The site is an homage organized by Shannon and Kenny of Wigtech.

Jayne County (www.jaynecounty.com) A rock-and-roll star who is "Man Enough to Be a Woman." Are you?

The Kids in the Hall (www.comedycentral.com/tv_shows/kith/) I love to watch the kids do female characters. You can see a tiny bit on this site or rent vintage *KITH* at your video store.

The Mangina (www.themangina.com) Artist who performs nude except for a self-made fake vulva. A sweet, wacky fellow.

Mother, NYC (www.mothernyc.com) Drag clubs, divas, and culture in New York City. Party planners and activists Chi Chi Valenti and Johnny Dynell, creators of the legendary Jackie's 60 and Mother clubs and events, keep the flame of tranny art alive. Visit their site that has links to all of the great drag performers (www.queenmother.tv). You can be kept abreast by subscribing to the drag events mailing. Their parties have the very best themes and are the most fun. Though her chromosomes would deny it, Chi Chi is definitely a drag mother. I could go on and on. . . .

Randy Constan aka Peter Pan (www.pixyland.org/peterpan) Truly the site of the boy who never grew up. Guitarist, inventor, and eternal child, Randy lives the life of Peter Pan and has the outfits to go with it. He also has his very own Tinkerbell. Click on My Fashion Pages, where there is a link to the Magic Wardrobe, where you can get your very own Tinkerbell costume from Anty Lyz.

The Rocky Horror Picture Show (www.rockyhorror.com) There are many sites dedicated to this inspiring drag and cult classic, but this site is the most popular. *Rocky Horror,* the creation of Richard O'Brien, began in London as a play, and it recently completed a successful Broadway revival run. If you are a sweet transvestite, you must see this movie, preferably at a midnight show, with you and everyone else dressing as characters. Have a blast!

RuPaul (www.rupaul.com) Rupaul shares the love. At Ru's site, check out the weblog and connect more personally with this brilliant and talented performer. And don't forget, you better work.

Sally's Hideaway (www.sallys-hideaway.com) The beautiful black-and-white photos by Brian Lantelme document the queens who dominated this funky, sexy NYC club from 1986–92 at their most glamorous.

Screaming Queens Entertainment (www.screamingqueens .com) Contact, Miss Understood. Looking for a human dessert table or some other fab concoction? Suitable for corporate events or bat mitzvahs.

Sisters of Perpetual Indulgence, Inc. (www.thesisters.org) Their weekly bingo game, like Rice-A-Roni, is a San Francisco treat. The sisters will also perform at your wedding, stage charity benefits, or hear your confession.

Too Tall Blondes (www.tootallblondes.com) Academy deans Miss Kate Bornstein and Miss Barbara Carrellas have many talents, and they travel.

Transgendered Guide to Las Vegas (www.geekbabe.com/dlv/lvthings.html) Las Vegas seems to be the perfect place for alternative lifestyles.

Trans Vamp (www.transvamp.com) Lovely tranny Kalina Isato's site has tons of great info and links that are free, plus pay-for-view pics. One of its strong points is the club-hopping section. Kalina is based in Philadelphia, so that area has the most details, but you can connect with places like Terre Haute, Indiana, too.

The WayOut Club, London (www.thewayoutclub.com) As in "way out of the closet." Each Saturday 200 to 300 trannies and friends from all over the planet convene at the WayOut Club party. More nights are contemplated. People hear of the club through the website, but also through the annual Tranny Guide (see publications). The parties are hosted by Vicky Lee, Steffan, and the highly energetic WayOut Girls. The website is the club's newsletter, so check it for updates. There are contests and shows galore.

Bridal

David's Bridal (www.davidsbridal.com) National chain with a huge selection, prices ranging from $99 to $1,000. Staff is very accommodating to trannies. See the site or call 800-399-BRIDE for their nearest location. They schedule fashion shows too! Print catalog available.

EBay Online Auctions (www.ebay.com) Ebay has lots of bridal gowns plus everything else you can imagine and some things you never thought of. But beware, it is the easiest place to totally lose track of the time.

Kathryn and Alexandra Historically Inspired Bridal Gowns (www.bridesandjokers.com) "If you can dream it, we can make it."

Sat'n Spurs Western bridal gowns (http://satnspurs.com/wdindex.htm) Some of the laciest and prettiest I have seen.

Trans Brides E-zine (www.transbride.freeola.net/index.htm) Website and magazine for transgendered brides and bridesmaids. A cluttered but comprehensive site with lots of photos from around the world and helpful links. Magazine features wedding planning tips.

Your Dream Gown (eroshop.com) A site specifically for trannies with some very elaborate gowns and very feminine, old-fashioned knickers.

Conventions and Conferences

There are many conventions and gatherings in the tranny world. To keep your calendar up-to-date, visit the International Foundation for Education website (www.ifge.org). You'll find out about such events as Southern Comfort and Be-All, and you will be surprised how many more there are. No need to sit at home alone in your room.

Corsetry

Long Island Staylace Society (www.staylace.com) Dedicated to corsetry, with copious resource links.

Versatile Fashions (www.versatile-fashions.com) There are other corset makers here and abroad, but I'm not best friends with them. Ms. Antoinette makes a great product, so why go elsewhere? They manufacture the Miss Vera tranny training corset and many other wasp-waisted styles. A print catalog is available from 714-538-0257.

Counselors and Therapists

American Association of Sex Educators, Counselors and Therapists (www.aasect.org) Provides referrals to certified sexuality counselors and therapists. These people really keep abreast of sex and gender issues.

Dr. Anne Lawrence (www.annelawrence.com) Anne Lawrence is a clinical psychologist. She is responsible for the website Transsexual Women's Resources (see medical). She is based in Seattle but also counsels by phone.

Dr. Marty Klein (www.sexed.org) Marty Klein is an author and lecturer. He publishes a provocative newsletter called *Sexual Intelligence*. I once appeared with him, along with a nymphomaniac and a necrophile, on the *Sally* show to help promote his book *Your Sexual Secrets*. My secret was I had no secrets. As for Marty, he's brilliant.

Samuel Kirschner (e-mail: intothepresent@aol.com) Mind/body counselor, New York, NY, 212-683-0219. One touch and he broadened Patti Harrington's horizons.

Your Sex Coach (www.yoursexcoach.com) Dr. Patti Britton is a smart, delightful woman. She is based in Los Angeles and does private counseling as well as counseling online.

Dance

Ballet (http://clubs.yahoo.com/clubs/balletcrossdressing) Site for male ballerina wanna-bes.

How to Strip (www.exoticdancelessons.com) How-to videos from Canada's best exotic dancers. Lessons in lap dancing and pole work. They also sell a CD-ROM on breast augmentation.

Les Ballets Trockadero de Monte Carlo (www.trockadero.org) An all-male ballet company that performs in drag, founded by choreographer Peter Anastos. The "Trocks" perform all over the world. The site has many beautiful photos and tons of tutus.

Dictionary

Frederick's of Hollywood Fashionary (www.fredericks.com) A dictionary of terms from "all-in-one" to "yarn-dyed." Just "Ask Amanda" and look for the Fashionary link.

Dresses and Gowns

Discount Dresses Online (www.discountdressesonline.com) Frumpy site but great prices and a nice selection of beaded gowns and more in all sizes.

Dresses.com by Odette Christiane (www.dresses.com) Evening, cocktail, and play clothes. I love these designs, though only a few are available so far in plus sizes. Lots of sexy stretchy fabrics. My favorite is their idea of "sportswear." I don't know what sports these girls are playing, but then, the company *is* in California.

Florence's Fashions, 68 Albion St., Wakefield, MA, 781-245-1385, Florence and Barbara Mirlocca, proprietors. No website, just a ladies' dress shop that opened its doors to trannies some years ago. Barbara also does transformations.

Loralie Gowns (www.Loralie.com) The prettiest prom dresses, from bouffant to slinky. Huge selection and great size information. Check it out just to feel pretty. Order online or available in shops across the United States (see site for locations).

Manhattan department stores   Lord & Taylor, Saks Fifth Avenue, Macy's, TJ Max, the deans and I take academy girls shopping in these stores all the time. They all have nice, big, private dressing rooms. We are always treated very courteously, especially when we loosen our purse strings.

Erotic

This is one area that needs more attention. There are just not enough images of trannies making love or in artistic yet blatantly provocative poses. Where are the tranny pleasure activists?

Amateur T-models   (www.femm.com) Webmistress Anna Christopher, plus lots of other volunteer vixens, in saucy poses.

Dita Von Teese   (www.dita.net) You girls need your female role models, and Dita is a great one. She is a pinup queen in the tradition of the forties, and she is also the very most popular fetish model and burlesque performance artist. She travels with her own Champagne glass and does a fan dance in toe shoes.

Mariette Pathy Allen   (www.mariettepathyallen.com) Our dean of photography, Mariette has been photographing the transgender movement for twenty-five years, and in that time she has taken some beautiful erotic photographs of individuals and couples.

Screw Magazine   (www.screwmag.com) *Screw*'s site is hard core and graphic, the sex scenes shot in explicit detail. To view the streaming movies, you must pay. The "she-male" stars are living Barbies, molded to perfection with silicone and surgery. If you are looking for hearts and flowers, this is not it—it is sex in the raw.

Siam Ladyboys (www.siam-ladyboy.com) This site introduces Kathoeys (as ladyboys are called in the language of Thailand), first in pretty travel photos and elegant native costume, then it gets down to business with explicit nudity. According to the site, Thailand boasts an above-average number of transsexuals and transvestites. It is the least expensive place for genital reassignment surgery.

Fashion Mags

Hint Magazine (www.hintmag.com) Online fashion mag with plenty of behind-the-scenes info and advice. For serious fashionistas.

Hotel Venus magazine (www.patriciafield.com) I almost listed this under "erotica" because of the gorgeous photography in this issue. So far, this is the first and only, volume 1, number 1. Hopefully there will be more. It is available online from the website or from the Hotel Venus and Patricia Field stores in New York City.

Supermodels (www.supermodels.it) I know there is one in each of you. Here's a site you can study from. Highlights the top models from the "supermodel era" of the late eighties/early nineties.

Vintage Harper's Bazaar (www.victoriana.com/library/harpers/vanderbilt.html) Link from this page to the December 15, 1877, issue, which describes Miss Vanderbilt's trousseau in exquisite detail. Follow the links to several other reprinted articles from the 1870s to 1890s.

Faux Furs

Fabulous Furs (www.fabulousfurs.com) Faux fur coats—the only kind Miss Vera's girls wear. Custom hem and sleeve lengths on the "Signature Line" they manufacture. Our bride Gayle cuddles in "fox" and "sable." Print catalog available.

Fetish and Exotic Wear

Dream Dresser (www.dreamdresser.com) "Everything you want. Nothing you need." Their motto sums it up. High-quality fetish wear. Free print catalog by subscription. There are two stores where you can shop in complete comfort, one in Washington, DC, at 1042 Wisconsin Ave., NW, and one in West Hollywood, at 8444–50 Santa Monica Blvd. For store hours call 800-96DREAM.

Foxy Lady Boutique This is a full-service clothing, wig, and shoe boutique. Lingerie is available in sizes small to 5X; beaded gowns from small to 8X; strippers' dresses and gowns from small to 3X; fetish wear (PVC and leather) from small to 4X; women's shoes from 6 to 17; women's boots from 6 to 15 (knee-high and thigh). In other words, they rise to any challenge. There is a print catalog but no website. The shop is at 2644 Mission St., San Francisco, CA, 415-285-4980.

Hotel Venus and Patricia Field (www.patriciafield.com) The designer made famous for her work on *Sex and the City* owns two stores that are tranny heavens. The fashions are hip and eclectic. In SoHo, Hotel Venus at 382 West Broadway also boasts a makeup and hair salon. The West Village shop, Patricia Field, where it all started, is positively Eighth Street.

LD Fashions: Sissy Fashions for Crossdressers (www.ldfashions.com) From Laura Walton, who is a cross-dresser and a model on the site: "LD Fashions has been in business for over 12 years. All of our fashions, dresses, petticoats and other accessories are designed and crafted by myself and my very close friend and partner, Diane. Diane actually taught me to sew and has over 25 years' experience designing and sewing clothing for cross-dressers and professional female impersonators. Most orders take 6 to 8 weeks to complete. In addition to our catalog items we also do custom designs."

Piedmont Boutique (www.piedmontsf.com) Outrageous fun fashions and accessories. Shop is located at 1452 Haight St. right in the heart of San Francisco's Haight/Ashbury, and the Haight may have calmed down, but Piedmont, thankfully, has not. Custom sizes and fabrics are available. You can still be a flowerchild in a psychedelic mini. For store hours, call 415-864-8075.

Purple Passion (www.purplepassion.com) Owner Hilton Flax is one of my favorite kinky people and a very respected member of the BDSM and leather communities. His store is his passion. Hilton loves latex but stocks it all: leather, corsets, PVC, shoes, boots, books, chain mail, toys, and more. His store is at 211 W. 20th St., New York, NY, and he spreads out a tranny welcome mat. Call 212-807-0486 for hours, or shop by appointment.

Stormy Leather (www.stormyleather.com) Leather and latex wardrobes. Motto: "Forbid yourself nothing." They offer a bridal and domme registry. What a nice idea! They also have a Lusty Line for plus sizes; beware the large cup sizes that accompany this line—you may have to stuff your bust. The store is at 1158 Howard St., San Francisco, CA. Call 415-626-1672 or 877-975-5577 for hours. The young woman we spoke with on the telephone was very helpful and accommodating.

Versatile Fashions (www.versatilefashions.com) Ms. Antoinette's kinky conglomerate has it all: PVC catsuits (she was the first to mass-market them), sexy minis, nurses' outfits, maids' uniforms, stockings, corsets, jewelry, breast forms—the works. Fab-u-lous. You can order direct or visit any of the retail stores across North America that offer her line. See the website or call 714-538-0257 for locations near you. Print catalogs are also available.

Foundation Garments

Frishman's (www.frish.com) See the description in Lingerie.

JC Penney (www.jcpenney.com) Believe it or not, you can find all your body building equipment and garments in their catalog.

Hair Removal

Advanced Electrology (www.advancedelectrology.com) Because follow-up appointments are needed, it's best to find an electrologist in your area. Dr. Mark Latina and Francine Capuzzo, R.N., welcome a transgendered clientele to their two Massachusetts locations, one in Woburn and one in Reading. They use the FDA-approved GentleLase Plus Laser and the Lightsheer Diode Laser.

The Art of Shaving (www.theartofshaving.com) This is a men's barbershop with a complete product line that turns beard removal into a gentle, sensuous experience and the perfect prelude to a makeover. There are three Manhattan locations and one in Dallas and one in Miami. All include barber services except the one on E. 62nd St. in New York City. Visit the site or call 800-493-2212 for exact locations.

Electrology 2000 (www.electrology2000.com) This more intense method of hair removal is designed to remove your beard in one year rather than the more usual two-year process, and if you're in a hurry, the trip to Carrolton, Texas, is worth it, says Miss Kate Bornstein. The owners are tranny Bren Piranio and her wife, Ruthann. Plan ahead; Electrology 2000 is usually booked in advance, but they do have cancellations. As you might imagine, some clients back out. The spirit is willing, but the flesh can be weak.

Electrolysis Referral Directory (www.electrolysisreferral.com) State-by-state guide to service providers with posted rates as well as contact info.

Institute of Laser Medicine (lasermedicine.org) You can find out more about laser hair removal at this California-based source.

International Guild of Professional Electrologists (www .igpe.org) Gives basic information on different methods and can help you find a service provider in your area through the Electrolysis Referral Directory.

Richard's Body Beautiful (www.body-beautiful.com) Richard is recommended by Manhattan hostess Glorya Wholesome. His shop is in the super-tranny-friendly East Village.

Stephanie Fischman, certified electrologist. Patti Harrington's specialist. Located in New York City. For an appointment, call 212-472-2491.

Herstory

Lee Brewster Memoriam (www.inch.com/~kdka/leegbrewster/inmemoriam.html) Bebe Scarpi's tribute as it appeared originally on the Lee's Mardi Gras website. An article by Jack Nichols appears at www.gaytoday.badpuppy.com/garchive/events/052500ev.htm and a reprint of the *New York Times* obituary by Douglas Martin is at www.yvonnesplace.net/news/leebrewster.html.

Newspaper account of Stonewall (www.yak.net/ian/stonewall.html) Reprint of the 1969 New York *Daily News* account of the police raid on the Stonewall Inn, which marked the beginning of the modern Gay Pride movement. Much attention is paid to the role trannies played in standing up to the police.

Remembering Our Dead (www.gender.org/remember) A list of those who died "because of hate and prejudice," created as a memorial by Gwendolyn Ann Smith and others, so that lives may be saved.

Stonewall Diary (www.inch.com/~kdka/stonewall/stone1.htm) Barbara Judith Marie's account that encompasses a movement. A labor of love and a fascinating read.

Transgender Forum Mall back-date publications (www.tgfmall.com/msbob/Mags_American.html) The magazines published by Lee Brewster (Drag), Kim Christy (Female Mimics), Jo Ann Roberts (Ladylike), and others are treasured sources of tranny herstory.

Transsexual, Transgender, and Intersex History (www
.transhistory.org) This site features information from the course of the
same name that Kay Brown teaches at the Harvey Milk Institute in San
Francisco.

Hosiery

Alex Blake Hosiery (www.alexblake.com) Hose, hose, hose, and a
hosiery club with automatic regular shipments.

L'Eggs Pantyhose (www.leggs.com) Become a L'Eggs insider and
rate new products. Sounds like the perfect job for you? (They keep their
list private.)

Magnolia Hosiery Mills, Inc. (www.magnoliahosiery.com)
Stockings only. One stocking enthusiast I know was such a good customer
they gave him a guided tour.

The Nylon Stocking Network (www.nylonstocking.net) Webmistress Nancy models her favorites for the pleasure of voyeurs and nylon
stocking enthusiasts.

Secrets in Lace (www.secretsinlace.com) Stockings, the kind that
stay up *and* are sexy, and sheer pantyhose are a specialty for this total
lingerie purveyor.

Hotels and Inns

The Bodhi Tree House (www.bodhitreeretreat.com) Every party
girl needs a place to relax and meditate with like-minded spirits. This is
it, located in Black Mountain, North Carolina. The innkeeper is Holly
Boswell, author and one of the organizers of the Southern Comfort Conference in Atlanta. Bodhi Tree refers to the name given to the tree where
Buddha found enlightenment. Don't worry, despite the woodsy location,
you're just a few minutes from shopping.

Gabriel's Guest House (www.bestinns.net/usa/ma/gabriels.html) Located in Provincetown, Massachusetts, where the Fantasia Fair takes place each fall. Not just a guest house, Gabriel's is also host to sex and gender workshops. 800-969-2643.

Hotel St. Augustine (www.hotelstaugustine.com) At a party in New York, I met the hip, gay owner of this great-looking deco hotel in South Beach, Miami, and he was happy to be included in this guide.

Inn on 23rd Street Bed and Breakfast (innon23rd@aol.com) 131 W. 23rd St., New York, NY, 212-463-0330. Where academy girls love to stay. Innkeeper Annette provides a lovely setting.

Jewelry

Ejools (www.ejools.com) Pearls and rhinestones, hair ornaments and tiaras.

Ron's Rhinestones (www.ronsrhinestones.com) Rhinestones are a tranny's best friend. Custom-designed rhinestone accessories. Total diamanté heaven, from tiaras to full dresses! Online catalog only.

Wedding Band Superstore (www.weddingbandsuperstore.com) A division of Houston Jewelry retail stores. Has a huge selection, great prices, and large sizes. This is where I ordered Gayle's and Hank's bands. The service was delightful.

Legal

Thomas: Legislative Information on the Internet (http://thomas.loc.gov) On this site you can check the status of a bill and see who's voting for what. Great for boys in heels who want to keep legislators on their toes.

Transgender Law & Policy Institute (www.transgenderlaw
.org/) Site maintained and updated by Paisley Currah, Brooklyn College,
CUNY. An advocacy group working on laws to advance transgender equality.

Transgender Legal (www.transgenderlegal.com) Phyllis Frye, an
out transgender attorney residing in Houston, has championed lesbian-
gay-bisexual-transsexual rights for twenty-five years. In 1991 she
founded the Transgender Law conference. She created this site to "accelerate the legal freedom of transgenders."

Transsexuals in Prison (www.transgender.org/tg/gic) Help for
trannies behind bars on such issues as prison rape and availability of hormones. (click on GIC TIP.)

Lingerie

Body Illusions (www.body-illusions.com) Sheer bra with pockets
for breast forms. Made specifically with you in mind, so you can wear your
breast forms and they will look real.

The Bra Experience (www.braexperience.com) Bras with invisible
straps so you can bare your shoulders and still bear your breasts.

Cameo-Intimates Lingerie (www.cameo-intimates.com) Great
vintage bra styles. Has home photos from customers.

Chiffon's TV Wardrobe (www.tvtimes.freeserve.co.uk/nighty2.htm)
A British site listed mainly for its great photos of vintage negligees. Links
to suppliers.

Comfilon (www.comfilon.com) Finally a company has manufactured
panty hose for men. They are not as sheer as ladies' hose, but they have
extra room where it counts. In sheer and opaque, and thigh-highs, too.

Fit for a Queen Fashions (www.fitforaqueenfashions.com) Garter belts. Super-sexy, dare I say, trashy outfits and thigh boots in large sizes. Though not everything is queen size.

Frishman's Intimate Apparel (www.frish.com) The website of the large store in the Bronx, New York. Expert staff on premises will custom-fit your retro and modern undergarments. Very tranny friendly.

Henry and June (www.henryandjune.com) Sexy sleepshirts, baby dolls, and peignoirs, and in plus sizes too.

Pre-owned Panties (www.pre-ownedpanties.com) Offers not just the panties but the pre-owned panties' owners' artwork. You can even sell your own pre-owned panties.

Secrets in Lace (www.secretsinlace.com) The owners are true lingerie enthusiasts and love finding quality items. Beautiful bras in all sizes.

Sulis Lingerie (www.sulis.co.uk) Pure silk and satin gowns from England. I love the NS 83 nightshirt. Delicious.

The Tiny Shop (www.tinyshop.com) Invisible straps that can be worn with your own favorite bras.

Victoria's Secret (www.victoriassecret.com) This national chain of retail stores gets high marks for making men feel comfortable when shopping for themselves.

Wonderbra (www.wonderbra.com) The site explains each style so you have an idea what to choose when you shop. Store locator is on the website.

Makeup and Cosmetics

A Discount Beauty Supply (www.adiscountbeauty.com) How can you live without eyelash bindis!

Alcon, NYC This tiny store at 235 W. 19th St. caters mainly to professionals and is great for hard-to-find supplies like Joe Blasco Blue Neutralizer #2 beard cover. 212-633-0551.

Asia Carrera (www.asiacarrera.com) This sassy porn star gives good instructions, using herself as a model. Excellent photographs.

Bliss World (www.blissworld.com) Bliss is the word when you visit their Manhattan spas. Some outrageously expensive items only a queen could afford.

Drag Queen Makeovers by Grae Phillips (www.graephillips.net) Available on CD and video. Also voice lessons with drag karaoke. Interactive CDs.

Eyebrowz (www.eyebrowz.com) Have eyebrows like a movie star using these helpful stencils.

Hotel Venus (www.patriciafield.com) At Hotel Venus, 382 West Broadway in SoHo, New York City, you can have your makeup applied with an airbrush and visit the hair "salon without limits."

Jim Bridges (www.jbridges.com) Jim has a shop in Hollywood and has made a great reputation traveling the tranny convention circuit. He's well loved.

Joe Blasco (www.joeblasco.com) Do you think you'd like to be a makeup artist? Joe Blasco, one of the greats, has established schools in

Hollywood and Florida. The website also offers products and great instructions.

Kevyn Aucoin (1962–2002)   (www.kevynaucoin.com) Makeup artist to the stars and producer of wonderful makeup books. Kevyn helped make the world a brighter place.

Life's a DRAAG   (www.draag.com) Makeovers by Tora Roberts, who is married to Jade, a cross-dresser. Tora's been catering primarily to the transgendered community for the last eight years in Vancouver, British Columbia. She also lists other makeup artists worldwide.

MAC Cosmetics   (maccosmetic.com) Even before RuPaul made them a household word, they made a complete line of great professional quality products.

MakeUp Mania   (www.makeupmania.com) This site makes you feel like you are gossiping in the makeup trailer on a Hollywood set. These are dedicated artists who stay up on the latest products, and you can too.

Mary Kay Cosmetics   (www.marykay.com) To find a consultant near you, contact the company via phone, 800-MARY KAY, or on their website.

My Fem Spirit   (www.myfemspirit.bigstep.com) Stephanie Robinson offers makeup and wig styling, among other things, in New York City.

Spa Cadet   (www.spacadet.com) Masks, muds, and more exotic items for body pampering. Have a ball.

TG Cosmetics   (www.tgcosmetics.com) Good instructions and a wide variety of products, but for a makeup site, it looks so tame. Definitely reaching out to a tranny clientele.

The Transgendered Girl Cosmetic Superstore (www .geocities.com/WestHollywood/Chelsea/1021/cosmetics.html) Run by tranny Bobbi, a smart little cookie with a lust for lipstick.

Medical

The Harry Benjamin International Gender Dysphoria Association, Inc. (HBIGDA) (www.hbigda.org) The professional organization devoted to the understanding and treatment of gender identity disorders. Approximately 350 members from around the world, in the fields of psychiatry, endocrinology, surgery, law, psychology, sociology, and counseling. Responsible for the Standards of Care, now in its sixth version. Bean Robinson, Ph.D., is the current executive director.

International Journal of Transgenderism (www.symposion .com/ijt) Scholarly journal with latest thinking.

St. James Infirmary (www.stjamesinfirmary.org) San Francisco medical clinic for sex workers, including tranny sex workers. Dr. Deb Cohan and staff have gotten rave reviews from Dr. Annie Sprinkle, our school sexologist.

The Transsexual Phenomenon (www.symposion.com/ijt/ benjamin) Dr. Harry Benjamin's entire book, published online. Some areas are a bit dated, but this is still a seminal work.

Transsexual Women's Resources (www.annelawrence.com/ twr) Everything you wanted to know about sex-reassignment surgery—all of the physical aspects involved in going from man to woman, complete with personal accounts and photos.

Movies

There are just so many, I decided to direct you to some places where you could read about many. Some of my personal m-f favorites (not in any particular order) are *Tootsie, Some Like It Hot, The Crying Game, The Cockettes, La Vie en Rose, Hairspray, The Adventures of Sebastian Cole, Just Like a Woman, Different for Girls, Glen or Glenda, Hedwig and the Angry Inch.*

Bright Lights Film Journal (www.brightlightsfilm.com) Editor Gary Morris reviews almost every tranny film.

Drag Link (www.draglink.com) Betty Bi is a hardworking tranny who is determined to be a cultural arbiter. She critiques movies, books, and more.

Gay & Lesbian film festivals Held in major cities in many states, these are the places to find most new films on bisexual and transgender themes.

Trannyfest (www.trannyfest.com) This San Francisco film festival grows more fascinating each year.

Nails

Beauty and Youth Salon 145 Seventh Ave. South, New York, NY. Funky but friendly. Patti's favorite.

Kiss Nails (www.kissusa.com) Kiss makes the self-adhesive nails that we love.

Talon Tru-tips (www.talon-sd.com) Artificial nails available in large and extralarge sizes for male hands.

Transvamp (www.transvamp.com) Kalina Isato tells how to polish.

News Sites

Gender Education and Advocacy Information Newsletter (www.gender.org) Publishes *GAIN*, Gender Advocacy Internet News.

Planet Out (www.planetout.com) Largest queer news and cultural source on the web. Tranny section hosts chats.

Novelties

Miniature finger panties (www.pre-ownedpanties.com/minipops/minipops.htm) Miniature panties "worn surreptitiously by business men and women the world over to reduce stress. . . . Don't be the only person in the room without a pair on your fingers."

Mysti Memories (www.mystimemories.com) Dolls, dolls, dolls. I know some of you have huge collections. Be sure to check out the Kingstate page, the doll that looks like a drag queen. Want to see my role model Katy Keene? They've got her as paper dolls.

One-Stop Surfing

Above & Beyond Gender Mall (www.abgender.com) "Very comprehensive and fairly classy," says student Christina Rosalita Starr, a surfer girl.

TG Now (www.tgnow.com) Says Christina, "TG Now seems to have the fastest set of links to resource materials (clothes, transformation services)." Very impressive.

Transgender Forum (www.tgforum.com) Great network of connections—articles, shopping, bulletin boards, and support groups database. One area of site is charged a fee, but there's a big free section.

Political

Feminists for Free Expression (FFEUSA.org) Deals with free speech issues, particularly relevant to women. I'm on the executive board.

Free Speech Coalition (www.freespeechcoalition.com) If you have an interest in adult entertainment, join this group.

International Foundation for Gender Education (IFGE) (www.ifge.org) Their website maintains an up-to-date listing for trans and trans-inclusive political groups, such as GenderPAC, It's Time America, and more. This is the transgender umbrella organization, with a calendar of the year's annual conferences and events and an excellent bookstore. Help support this vital resource by becoming a member.

Publications

Atomic magazine (www.atomicmag.com) A magazine of retro culture with modern pinups done in retro style. You'll love the "Atomic girls." Created by Jeff Griffith, who also designed our award-winning ads.

Girl Talk magazine (www.girltalkmag.com) Gina Lance is the editor.

Greenery Press (www.greenerypress.com) Publishers of *The Lazy Crossdresser* and other tranny themes.

International Journal of Transgenderism (www.symposion .com/ijt) Scholarly journal publishes research papers online. Keeps you up-to-date on this fast-moving subject. Offers contact info on its contributors and advisers.

Ladylike magazine (www.cdspub.com/LL.html)

Simply Gorgeous Magazine (www.simplygorgeousmag.com) This is a new and very sexy magazine, centering on New York City.

The Tranny Guide (www.wayout-publishing.com) My very favorite tranny mag. It's an international guide of clubs, products, and services for the tranny planet plus helpful articles. Put out annually by Ms. Vicky Lee and the wonderful WayOut Club in London. They've got great tranny attitude. *Tranny Guide* rocks! Available at hip bookstores in the United States and online.

Transgender Community News (www.ren.org/tcn.html) Monthly magazine published by Renaissance.

Rather than listing tranny classics, I prefer you go to these sites. Reviews both capsule and longer are offered.

CDS Bookstand (www.cdspub.com) One of those great sites with tons of offerings, including archival magazines.

IFGE Bookstore (www.ifge.org) The tranny B&N. Plus every purchase helps a great group.

Religion

Metropolitan Community Church (www.ufmcc.com/perrybio.htm) Church founded in 1968 by Rev. Elder Dr. Troy D. Perry, an openly gay clergyman, in order to offer a religious congregation to those who might be excluded from others, in particular gays, lesbians, bisexuals, and transgendered persons, their families, and their friends. From Rev. Perry's living room it has expanded to 44,000-plus people in more than 300 congregations in 17 countries around the world.

Through the Cracks Ministries (www.throughthecracks.org) Started by Randy Constan aka Peter Pan, for those who feel they have fallen through the cracks of organized religion.

Resource Centers

Gay and lesbian centers, though they may not yet have changed their names to include transgender services, actually do. There are centers in

Atlanta; Long Beach, CA; Orange County, CA; San Francisco; and southern Arizona, to name a few.

Ingersoll Gender Center (www.ingersollcenter.org) Founded in 1977, this Puget Sound area nonprofit center offers a wide range of services, including counseling and support groups. 1812 E. Madison St., Seattle, WA, 206-860-6064.

New York Lesbian, Gay, Bisexual, Transgender Community Center (www.gaycenter.org) A hotbed of social, political, educational, and cultural activity; cultural, counseling, and social services; education and outreach, recreation, and public policy.

Scents

Fleur de Leigh (www.fleurdeleigh.com) You know I love that name. They offer a scent-of-the-month club, which sounds delicious, and their bubble bath bubbles.

Pheromones (www.apconcentrate.com) To go with your faux vulva, perhaps. Attract men or women with these scents. So it sounds like a crazy idea—well, it won't be the first that we've tried.

Self-Defense

The Cop Shopper (www.cop-shopper.com) Plastic and metal police whistles. Storm whistles are the loudest.

The Music House (www.themusichouse.com) Besides offering a beautiful music box collection, this site has serious whistles. Offers the Thunderer by Acme, a real screamer, and "Bobby" whistles like British police use. Site is equipped with audio samples.

National Coalition of Anti-Violence Programs
(www.avp.org) The URL takes you to the New York City Gay & Lesbian Anti-Violence Project. Click on "NCAVP" to get to the national listings.

Sex Education

Betty Dodson (www.bettydodson.com) Dr. Betty's website will one day be considered a part of folk history. Explicit, educational, and fun.

Bi the Way (www.bitheway.org) Very thorough listing of resources for bisexuals.

Good Vibrations (www.goodvibes.com) The Good Vibrations sexuality boutique in San Francisco is a community treasure, home to toys and to publications from the Sexuality Library.

Grand Opening Boutique (www.grandopening.com) Kim Airs has created a safe space not just for shopping but also for learning.

Harvey Milk Institute (www.harveymilk.org) In San Francisco, a community-based learning institution with courses ranging from trans history to "Butt Play: A Hands-In Approach." Classes at various SF locations.

Loving More (www.lovemore.com) The Loving More organization is dedicated to those who want to pursue committed relationships involving more than one person.

Museum of Menstruation and Women's Health
(www.mum.org) Director, Harry Finley. If I had put it under "Medical," would you have found it?

Museum of Sex (www.mosex.com) The Museum of Sex, based in New York City, will have its inaugural exhibit in fall 2002, and it's cause for celebration. May the museum prosper; it's sorely needed.

Sex Muse Erotic Art Gallery   (sexmuse.net) Erotic art to inspire your imagination, and all of it for sale. The first tranny artist to be offered was Pet Silvia.

Society for Human Sexuality   (www.sexuality.org) Based in Seattle, this group offers an online library of writings from some of the best modern sex thinkers.

Tristan Taormino   (www.puckerup.com) Ms. Taormino, by way of her books, her *Village Voice* column, and her penetrating observations, has made anal sex a household word.

Shoes

Debbi's Hose & Heels   (www.geocities.com/WestHollywood/ Village/7740/debbishoesnewa.html).

Fit for a Queen Fashions   (www.fitforaqueenfashions.com/large_ size_shoes) Shoes with seven-inch heels, glitter and glow-in-the-dark platforms, and pumps. Up to size 17.

Italian Heels   (www.italianheels.com) Very high heels, especially sandals, in large and custom sizes. Priced in euros, so subject to changes in the exchange rate.

Leslie Shoe Company   (www.sexyshoe.com) "Your high-heel specialists." Need I say more?

Maryland Square   (www.marylandsquare.com) Has a large selection of "real girl" shoes. Everyday practical styles, not fetish wear. Sizes 6 to 14 in widths N through WW. The company has a great reputation for service. Every woman with feet needs to know about this site. Print catalog can be requested on the website.

Sissy Sites

Note, some of these sites carry the warning label (ff) for "forced femi-nization." It's not my style, but we all have to start somewhere, and if this helps you get in touch with your feelings, it's better than being isolated. In each listed, there is also much cleverness involved and more than an occasional girlish giggle.

House of Sissify.com (www.sissify.com/home.html) Pretty and pink (ff).

Our Way magazine (www.bobbiswan.com) Bobbi Swan is one hardworking maid. She's been publishing this mag for nine years, the last four online. Stories and photos from sissy maids around the world.

The Pinafore Pages (www.pinaforepages.com) Training for hus-bands. Directed at wives (yeah, right) to help you ease your husband out of his fear of wearing a bra and get him into an apron (ff).

Social and Support

Crossdressers International (http://members.tripod.com/~CDINYC/). Located in New York City, 212-570-7389.

Fantasia Fair (www.fantasiafair.org) During this weeklong celebra-tion, the town of Provincetown, Massachusetts, is pretty much taken over by transgenderists. Now in its twenty-seventh year, Fanstasia Fair is fan-tastic. Unfortunately, Fantasia Fair takes place in the autumn, so you won't be wearing your new maillot at the beach.

Financing Transition for Transsexual Women (www.tsroadmap.com/reality/finance) Andrea James gives detailed budget ad-vice in workbook form, covering all aspects of transition costs.

Gennation, Ltd. (www.thirdgenesis.com/gennation) Would you feel more comfortable with a new ID card? It's offered here. Just be sure to carry your legal ID with you too.

The International Foundation for Gender Education (www.ifge.org) When I first started the academy, the existence of this group made life a lot easier. It's a tremendous resource, a tranny umbrella organization—community-based support group info, events calendar, bookstore. Publishes *Transgender Tapestry* magazine. Deserves everyone's support.

Pretty T-girls (www.transgenderdir.com) Says Chrissy Starr, "Susana Marques's massive directory has been around for a long time and keeps getting bigger. It must be the most comprehensive listing of T-girls' home pages and websites. Of course, size means a range of quality."

The Renaissance: Transgender Organization (www.ren.org) Education and support group. Also publishes a monthly magazine, *Transgender Community News*.

T Girls Network (www.tgirls.net) Conducts T-girl-of-the-month contest. The Vanity Club, which has its home here, is an online club with fun photo sets and even recipes from T-girl members. My favorite was Betty's Pop Tarts.

Transgender Support Site (http://heartcorps.com/journeys) Melanie Anne Phillips shares what she has learned on her tranny journey and it is plenty. She also founded the transgender community forum on AOL.

Tri-Ess: The Society for the Second Self (www.triess.org). National support and social organization of heterosexual cross-dressers and their families and loved ones with chapters across North America.

URNotAlone (www.urnotalone.com) A site that manages to be "respectable and sexy," according to the article in the *Rosebuds* newsletter of the Tiffany club (www.tcne.org). This is a meeting place where trannies and their admirers can post photos and profiles. There is also an escort section. Lots of free sections and an adult pay section.

Social and Support—Kids

CD-Kids (www.geocities.com/SouthBeach/Plateau/2476) Support for children of cross-dressers.

Mermaids: Family Support Group for Children and Teenagers with Gender Identity Issues (www.mermaids .freeuk.com) Also offers support to their parents. Sells the Mermaid calendar made by the kids. Loosely associated with Britain's National Health Service.

Transproud (www.transproud.org) Site for transgender youth. Part of OutProud, national coalition for gay, lesbian, bi, and transgender youth.

Trans Youth and their families (www.annelawrence.youngindex .html) A page on the Transsexual Women's Resources site. Here you'll find links to sites such as Sarah's Room.

Social and Support—Wives and Partners

Rainbow Trail (www.rainbowtrail.info/) Online group for significant others.

SPICE (Spouses and Partners International Conference for Education) (www.tri.ess.org/spice) Annual meeting of wives and families of cross-dressers. (Husbands may attend, but not in drag.) Held in July.

The Sweetheart Connection (www.rainbowtrail.info/) The SPICE newsletter. This site introduces the editor and gives subscription information on how to get it snail mail.

T & A and Other Body Parts

body-illusions.com Sells Mystique ($269) attachable breast forms. Not a huge catalog, but well-thought-out quality items.

Castle Supply (www.castlesupplys.com) Offers latex vaginas and related accessories. Even offers a Menstrual Kit for once-a-month ultra-realness. FYI, I did try to contact them by phone and never got a call back, but I do see their products offered around the net and they certainly seem worth investigating. It's not like pussies grow on trees.

Classic Curves International (www.clcrv.com) Besides the Diva bra, tranny Espy Lopez designed a hip-enhancement undergarment and named it Veronica, so you know I have a warm place in my heart for her. I like that thong gaff, "the showgirl's secret," and It Stays, the body glue that will hold up your bra straps. If you want to get on Espy's good side, send her a pair of tap pants. She loves them.

C.P. Mart (www.cpmart.com) Has great selection, including hip pads in different sizes and excellent sizing charts for breast forms. I like the look of the Panty Plus padded panty.

Tranny Emporiums

The following shops offer one-stop shopping for tranny basics such as breast forms, wigs, makeup, clothing plus, in some cases, books and magazines.

Changes TV Boutique (www.changestvboutique.com) New retail store in Manhattan owned by tranny Frank/Leslie. 581 Ninth Ave., 646-473-0184.

The Glamorous Woman   (www.theglamorouswoman.com)

Glamour Boutique   (www.glamourboutique.com) They have two bricks-and-mortar locations (one in Massachusetts and one in Las Vegas) as well as the online store.

Jim Bridges Boutique   (www.jbridges.com) The tranny's friend, Jim has probably transformed more trannies than anyone. He is a familiar sight at conventions and gets those girls looking pretty in no time. He has a lovely boutique and makeover salon in sunny California and an online department store.

Lydia's Transgender Fashions   (www.lydiastv.com) Retail store and transformation salon in Los Angeles plus online. These lovely people, Paul, a CD, and his wife, Kathy, an experienced cosmetologist, are celebrating twenty years in the transformation business. My student Jill came back from a visit to Lydia's with a glowing report. Lockers available for your home away from home. Located in a motel, which makes it all the more fun. No sleep-overs, but a social lounge.

Transformation Shops (U.K.)   (www.transformation.co.uk) Chain of six retail shops in the U.K. and branches in Ireland and Germany founded by Stephanie Anne Lloyd, a transsexual woman. Salon and online product line. All shops provide the whole range of products, magazines, videos, and services that are totally unique and exclusive to Transformation.

Transformation Specialists

Fakeovers: Virtual Makeovers for Crossdressers and More . . .   (www.geocities.com/fakeovers) This site encourages you to use the Cosmopolitan makeover software to complete your own virtual transformation, then post it in the site's gallery. If you don't think you can accomplish this yourself, right now the site is looking for models, so you can send your before photo in and they'll do the after.

Florence's Fashion   68 Albion St., Wakefield, MA 01880, 781-245-1385. Proprietress Barbara Mirlocca. No website.

Teach Yourself How to Be a Drag Queen 101 with Sherry Vine   (Video available at www.eastvillageproductions.com) I've loved Sherry Vine ever since I saw her in *Charlie*, a sort of combo *Charlie's Angels*/Charles Manson melodraga. A talented New Yorker, she's often called abroad to perform.

TgNOW   (www.tgnow.com) This site has a great list of service providers across the country. At last count there were about fifty.

Voice

How to Develop a Female Voice   (www.heartcorps.com/journeys/voice.htm) Melanie Anne Phillips. Tips on voice. Also available as a VHS or audio CD.

Judith Pollack   (www.missvera.com/faculty) The academy's dean of voice conducts private tutorials for serious-minded students.

Transsexual Voice   (www.tsvoice.com) Speech therapy training. Offers free online tutoring in voice transformation and audio samples on the site.

Wigs

Barry Hendrickson's Bitz N Pieces   This is actually a wig and millinery salon. A lovely, airy space in which the goodies stand out against the clean white walls. Talented staff is headed by Gwen when Barry lounges in Florida. A wall of celebrity photos attests to their expertise. Located at 1841 Broadway, Suite 201, New York, NY, 212-397-0711.

Wig Salon   (www.wigsalon.com) Offers wigs for girls with big heads—and don't we all know a few of those!

Wigtech NYC (www.wigtech.com) Shannon Harrington is in command of the tresses here. Your wig can come styled in one of many different coifs, from Marilyn to Marie Antoinette to the most up-to-the-minute looks. Shannon, who is in charge of the academy's do's, says, "If I wouldn't wear it myself, I won't sell it to you, honey."

www.wigs.com   Recommended by Chrissy Starr.

Your Own Web Page

Yahoo Geocities (http://geocities.yahoo.com/home) Many trannies have their very own web pages. Why not you? Yahoo hosts the most popular community at present, and its instructions are easy.

Miss Vera's Finishing School for Boys Who Want to Be Girls

(www.missvera.com; e-mail webhostess@missvera.com or crossdress @missvera.com) Miss Vera's is a dream come true, and we are also a very real school. You can visit us for on-campus classes or study online, via telephone, or all three. You have so much to learn! Our brochure and enrollment application are available online (e-mail webhostess@missvera.com, or crossdress@missvera.com) or you may write to us at P.O. Box 1331, Old Chelsea Station, New York, NY 10011 or telephone the academy office, 212-242-6449, and the information packet will be sent to you discreetly.

Cherchez la femme,

Veronica Vera

Veronica Vera
Dean of Students

Veronica Vera is the author of *Miss Vera's Finishing School for Boys Who Want to Be Girls* and has written hundreds of articles on human sexuality. She is a sex workers' rights activist and is on the board of Feminists for Free Expression. A former adult movie star, she has traveled, performed, and lectured around the world. She lives in New York City.